Great Things Happen Every Day

Finding joy with family, friends and banana milkshakes

PHIL BARTH

Copyright © 2019 Phil Barth

All rights reserved.

ISBN: 9781079162202

DEDICATION

To my wife Beth and my three sons Kenny, Joe and Tommy. Of many great things that have happened to me in my life, you are the greatest.

Speaking of my wife and one of my sons: Credit for the cover photo goes to my wife Beth. The picture of our son Tommy was taken on vacation at Isle of Palms, South Carolina in June 2017.

CONTENTS

1	Why Am I Writing This Book?	3
2	Great Family Traditions	11
3	The Annual Family Vacation	27
4	Day Trips	37
5	Shopping – Kohl's and More	41
6	Day Camp	49
7	The World Championship of Public Speaking	55
8	Sea Base	67
9	Let's Eat! And Exercise	73
10	The Recipes	89
11	Humor	109
12	Dad Jokes	131
13	Pets	137
14	Great Moments, Great People	147
15	Miscellaneous Stories	159
16	Conclusion	175

ACKNOWLEDGMENTS

I have already acknowledged my wife and family in the dedication. But without them the great things never happen, and the book never happens.

Michael Davis (Speaking CPR) is my speaking / storytelling coach. The larger stories that are in this book, as well as the stories I tell in my speeches are better because of what I've learned from him. (If they still suck, just think how bad they'd be if I hadn't learned from him).

Greg Walker (the Big Dreamer) has inspired people worldwide. As a friend, fellow speaker and fellow author you inspire me daily.

My Facebook friends have given me constant feedback on Great Things. I see people on the street and they tell me "I love hearing the great things!" Without that feedback I don't think I would have kept going. I love you all.

Mom, dad and my late grandma Tots - thanks for never putting limits on me. I never once heard "You can't do that!" from any of you. Not when it came to achieving goals (like writing books, winning speech contests and more).

Kenny and Joyce Craig (my father in law and mother in law) have been responsible for a huge number of great things in this book and in my life (and Beth's life). Whether it was holidays, vacations, or just a conversation and beer by the pool.

1 | WHY AM I WRITING THIS BOOK?

On August 5, 2015 I took a surprise trip to the cardiac wing of Bethesda North Hospital in Cincinnati. I suffered what was labeled a "small" heart attack. I remember thinking "If this is small I'd hate to see medium."

(Side note: if they labeled heart attacks like Starbucks - tall, grande and venti - I think people could relate better. "You had a 'tall' heart attack." "Yep, sounds about right…")

I then thought "This can't happen to me. I'm only 52 years old. There is no history of heart issues in my family. I'm not lean and trim, but I'm only ten pounds (or so) overweight.

"The timing is all wrong. Next week I'm supposed to speak at the semi-finals of the World Championship of Public Speaking in Las Vegas!"

Somehow none of that mattered to my heart.

On August 6, 2015, I received two stents. Two of my smaller arteries were blocked (one 95% another 80%).

The surgeon visited me in recovery. We talked for a while and somehow the subject of stress came up. I think he brought it up. I don't like to talk about stress.

I don't remember everything he said, but I do remember two things clearly.

"Whatever it is, it's not worth the stress (whatever "it" is)" and "You need to unplug for one week every three months".

A week later I met my cardiologist, Dr. Brooks Gerlinger. If you're in the Cincinnati area and ever need a cardiologist I highly recommend him. Despite what you're going to read next.

Dr. Gerlinger said "It was a small artery and we fixed it. But if you don't want to come back, you need to cut back on three things."

"First: Caffeine."

Wow did this one hurt. In December 2014 I got a Keurig for Christmas. I used it to make a quick cup of coffee in the morning while the full pot was brewing.

"One cup of regular coffee per day. And No Starbucks."

He wasn't done. "Second: Do you drink?"

After losing my Starbucks? Yeah!

"You can have one to two small glasses of red wine per day. But if you save them up during the week, on Saturday you get (pause) one to two small glasses of red wine."

"Third: You need Less Stress."

With no Starbucks and a thimble of Merlot? Right.

"Stress can block arteries. Including the one we call the Widowmaker." (Did you know you have an artery named the Widowmaker? Even if you're not married!)

"Phil, Do you know what happens if you have a blocked Widowmaker?"

"I can guess".

"Right. You fail at your goal of not dying."

WHY AM I WRITING THIS BOOK?

I thought "Wine – okay. Coffee – I can try. But why do people keep talking about stress? I don't stress. I know people who stress about health – I don't even think about it!"

That was a clue.

"Stress? Come on. I'm killing it. I've got a job, scouts, church, Toastmasters, travel, and teenagers. I don't have time for stress! I just keep it all inside."

That was really a clue.

The clues were in front of me and I was ignoring them. But when Dr. Gerlinger said "Widowmaker", I listened.

Especially when he said it in front of my wife!

The rest of 2015 was a fairly low stress time. I took the time needed to recover – including exercise therapy - through early December. Christmas is always a low stress time with family.

In January I was back at work full time. I committed to one unplugged week every three months. Naturally, I waited until the end of March to do it.

The last week of March was our youngest son Tom's spring break. I took a week of vacation. One of the nice things about having worked for one company as long as I have is the vacation. I get six weeks.

We started "unplugged week" with a family trip to the Cincinnati Zoo.

At the end of the day I got on Facebook (I didn't unplug from everything) and listed the great things that happened on the day:

- Watched the gorillas at the zoo.
- Saw the new baby cheetahs (also at the zoo).
- Had a picnic lunch in the car with Beth and Tommy - a little too cold to do the picnic area....
- Watched Tommy feed a giraffe.
- A nap in the hammock (it's still indoors).

GREAT THINGS HAPPEN EVERY DAY

- Elliptical at the YMCA.
- Dinner at my in-laws - I provided the grilled chicken.
- The new grilled chicken recipe (Coca Cola chicken) was a hit.
- Banana milkshakes before bed.
- Found a new area rug for the family room online - free after Kohl's cash.

The next day I decided to try it again:

- Went to the art museum with Beth and Tommy.
- Saw some great works of art.
- Also saw some things that made me laugh out loud...
- Shrimp and grits for lunch.
- Mowed the grass - lawnmower started no problem after a winter's rest.
- Taco night for dinner!
- Took a walk with Beth after dinner.
- Found Tom a Chinese drawing set on Amazon.

On the third day of vacation I entered more great things:

- Shoulder therapy - I keep getting better range of motion.
- Shot some baskets in the driveway - the therapy is working!
- Ran two miles.
- Tom came along with me on the run and rode his scooter.
- La Rosa's for dinner - spaghetti and salad.
- Fixed the clogged drains.
- Mowed more of the lawn.
- Got over 17,500 steps in for the third day in a row.
- Got the cistern filter cleaned.
- Watched a Big Bang Theory rerun with the family.

By March 31 I decided that I could to it for the whole week. I had the time off, so why not?

- 30 minutes on the stationary bike tonight.
- The fact that I was able to catch my mistake on the prior item and not have people thinking I was riding a bike made out of fancy paper.

WHY AM I WRITING THIS BOOK?

- 30 minutes of Zig Ziglar's Born to Win while I rode the bike.
- Our new inflatable solar powered camping lights arrived from Amazon

Some time before Friday I had a thought: What if I kept going with the great things list? On work days? On every day? Even work days? How long could I keep finding great things?

I decided to try it for another week. Then a month. Then... well I'm still doing it four years later.

Before long I was capturing great things with pictures or quick notes. I started to look for the great things in life during the day. I found them. Every day. Well, almost every day. (We'll get to that).

While finding great things lowered my stress, just looking for great things in life lowered my stress. After my heart attack I started exercising more. I cleaned up my diet. I lowered my caffeine intake, cut my salt, and (sigh) cut my wine consumption.

I believe the biggest change I made, the change that kept me away from a return trip to the cardiac wing of Bethesda North Hospital in Cincinnati, is the drop in stress.

THE DROP IN STRESS COMES DIRECTLY FROM MY DAILY PRACTICE OF LISTING GREAT THINGS.

In May 1957 Scientific American Magazine published an article "The Reticular Formation" that discussed the brain's Reticular Activating System.

I'll save you the science, except for one experiment: Think of the color red. Tell yourself to notice the red all around you. Now look around. Amazing how much red is around you, right?

Even more amazing is the fact that your mind will keep bringing you red things all day, unless... Unless you tell yourself to notice green. Then the world turns green.

Whatever you tell your mind to focus on, you will get. And you'll get a lot of it.

When I started listing great things I had no idea that I was activating my brain's Reticular Activating System. In fact I had no idea that I even had a Reticular Activating System.

But the more great things I listed, the more great things I found, and the more great things I listed.

You get to choose your focus. There are plenty of ways to complain about why life sucks, why people with differing opinions are idiots, why some or all politicians (depending on your point of view) are crooks and liars, why the New England Patriots are awful (okay, that's my opinion), etc.

All of those complaints are excellent ways to raise your stress hormones.

Or... you can decide to look for the green. You can look for the areas where life is great. You can see the value in all people, even people with differing opinions. You can even appreciate the Patriots. (I can't, but you can).

That's why I'm writing this book. I want to start a movement where we focus on what's great in life. I want to start a lower stress movement. I want to keep one person out of the cardiac wing. I want that person to be you.

YEAH, BUT WHY BANANA MILKSHAKES?

Shortly after my heart attack we bought a Nutri Bullet as part of my diet cleanup.

Nutri Bullets make delicious smoothies. The idea (according to the maker of the Nutri Bullet) is to mix half fruits and half vegetables in a delicious and nutritious smoothie. And the idea works well, except for that whole vegetable thing.

WHY AM I WRITING THIS BOOK?

You put one kale leaf in there and the whole thing tastes like dirt. I can tolerate spinach, but I find that spinach works best in a salad – if I'm going with veggies, I commit.

After expressing my vegetables in smoothies frustrations with my wife, she said "What about banana milkshakes? We used to have them as kids. We could make them with vanilla frozen yogurt and low fat milk." I'd never heard of banana milkshakes, but I noticed that her recipe had no vegetables in it, so I said "Let's give it a try."

Banana milkshakes are delicious.

And they're simple.

And they're memorable.

That makes them the essence of a great thing. It can be small, but it's wonderful. It makes your heart happy (especially if you use low fat frozen yogurt).

The rest of this book is broken into sections of great things. As I recorded great things over time I noticed that many of them fell into categories. Categories like family traditions and celebrations, vacations and other adventures.

Some great things were as small as a trip to the grocery store or a Flea Market. Some were as large as a week in the Florida Keys or a trip to Chicago to compete for the Toastmasters World Championship of Public Speaking.

Sometimes the great thing was a person I met. Sometimes it was something funny. (Or, in the case of "dad jokes" something I found funny). Frequently it was something to do with one of our pets.

And sometimes, the great thing was someone else starting their list of great things.

I hope you start a list as well. You don't have to put the list on Social Media. You don't even need to write it down. Just think about the great things that happened each day.

That said, if you'd like to write it down, I'd love to hear from you. If you have a great family tradition, great recipe or any other great moment that makes life more enjoyable - send them to me on Twitter (@philbarthspeaks), or shoot me an e-mail – phil@philbarthspeaks.com. I will in turn share the greatest things on my website (www.philbarth.com)

Without further ado, here are some of the great things that happened every day.

Okay – one little bit of ado:

The Kindle version of this book (written first) has all kinds of hyperlinks. Those don't work so well in a paperback book. For the most part I left the links in this book – they can be typed in. But… if you want the ease of clicking on the link you have two options:

I included the Kindle book for free on Amazon when you buy the paperback – you can pick it up on Amazon, or

You can go to my website (www.philbarth.com) and find the links on the front page.

2 | GREAT FAMILY TRADITIONS

On the morning of July 4, 1995 I was sound asleep in bed. Beth and I were a week or so away from being new parents. At least that's what the Doctor told us on Beth's July 3 checkup: She was due on July 9, but would probably go a little late.

So it came as a bit of a surprise when Beth woke me up at 7:00 and said "Sweetie, my water broke."

I went in to turbo mode. "Do I have time to get a shower? (Yes) Are we packed? (Nope - we were going to do it after the cookout that day). Does your sister's idiot boyfriend have July 4 in the pool? (Yes)".

That evening, as the fireworks went off we had our first precious bundle of joy - Kenneth John Barth. 24 years later he is a guitar playing wizard. He can also play trombone, piano, drums (and a bunch of other instruments) but guitar is his first love.

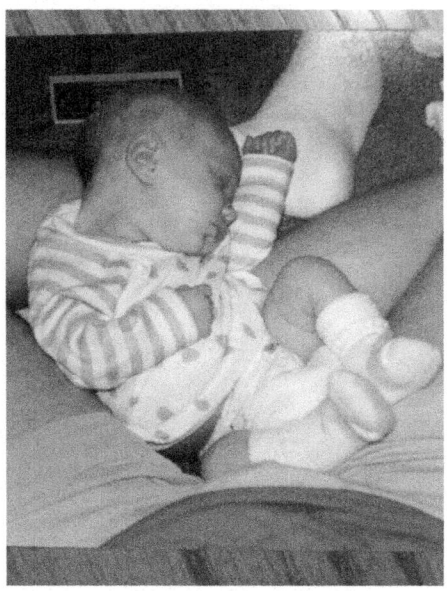

Guess I saw his guitar abilities at a young age...

GREAT THINGS...
KENNY'S BIRTHDAY - JULY 4, 2016

- The kids got chicken and potato wedges from Medary's for lunch.
- Beth made chicken salad for the two of us.
- Kenny and I washed down our lunch with an IPA from The Old Firehouse Brewery.
- I smoked two racks of ribs for six hours.
- Beth's sister Paige and her parents came over for Kenny's birthday dinner: Ribs, brats, metts, hot dogs, tater tots, baked beans, watermelon, deviled eggs, hummus.
- And a really good birthday cake for dessert.
- Opened a howler of raspberry ale (from The Old Firehouse Brewery).
- Got a 10-minute nap in while I did the ribs.
- Got a 20-minute nap in after dinner.

Kenny always has one request for his birthday dinner: Ribs. That is a request I can live with.

The great thing about having a son with a July 4 birthday (besides the fact he gets a fireworks display every birthday): Every July 4 Jungle Jim's has baby back ribs on sale for about than $2.79 per lb. I like smoking ribs. I have yet to note a rib smoking session that didn't include a nap.

Joseph Craig Barth joined our family on May 23, 1998. This was roughly three weeks before he was due. Once again, the two project managers were caught a little off guard by the new completion date.

That said, he weighed in at 8 lb 3 oz. Three weeks early was just fine.

Joe is also a fantastic guitar player. He and Kenny both play in the Metal band Starless.

https://www.facebook.com/strlesscincy/

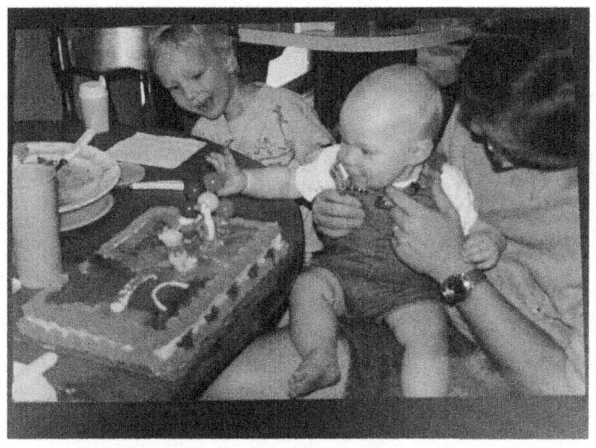

JOE'S BIRTHDAY - MAY 23, 2016

- Joe's 18th birthday party with family and friends.
- Smoked ribs, smoked chicken (a first), hot dogs, brats and metts for the main course.
- Beth's pumpkin pie for dessert!
- While I was doing the ribs I had enough time to put away the camping equipment and take a power nap.
- Happy birthday to my hilarious son Joe!

Joe keeps me on my toes. Come to think of it all my sons do. But Joe literally keeps me on my toes sometimes: From the time at age 1 when he stood in the stroller at Kohl's to the time at age 4 when Beth's grandma called and asked "Is your mom there?". Joe said "Yes she is!" and hung up.

And then there's the nerf dart wars... more on that later.

Our last Christmas present of 2001 arrived two days late. On December 27, Thomas Robert Barth was born.

At this point, I knew the drill. We would go to the hospital and two days later come home with a blue eyed blonde haired boy.

We knew for sure we would have a boy. I was basing the hair and eye prediction on history. Both of the other babies were born with blonde hair and blue eyes.

And sure enough, we had a boy. A brown haired brown eyed boy. Looks just like his mom, the lucky guy.

We love having a Christmas baby. Tom gets double presents (separated by a day off). Sometimes we take Tom's birthday party on the road. That was the case in 2018. At the time I needed one more night at a Hilton property to move up to the next reward level for 2019.

NOTE: I'm not saying the Hilton reward level was what drove the decision to take the party on the road. It was just a happy coincidence.

We gave Tom a map and said "Pick something within two to three hours driving distance (Dayton, Cincinnati, Lexington, Louisville, Columbus, Indianapolis)". He chose Indianapolis. I booked a room at Embassy Suites and we were all set.

As a side note, Tom lobbied hard for a longer driving distance limit (so we would add Chicago to the mix). After hearing about our World Championship of Public Speaking Chicago adventure Tom put it on his bucket list.

I told him that December in Chicago might not be quite as fun as he was imagining, and a summer trip to Chicago would be a better option. He agreed.

TOM'S BIRTHDAY PARTY – DECEMBER 27, 2018:

- We drove to Indianapolis.
- We stopped about ten miles from the hotel, and it was the same exit where Beth and I used to shop: Castleton Square Mall.
- Tom found a copy of the game Munchkin Deluxe half off.
- Beth found a jigsaw puzzle.
- We had liquid nitrogen created ice cream. Very cool (-321 F to be exact).
- Then Beth hit Kohl's while Tom and I hit a game store. We bought four games.
- Tom and I found some ties at Kohl's (Two Christmas and two Jerry Garcias). Beth found a nice sweater.
- We made it to Embassy Suites in time for Happy Hour.
- Then we had dinner at Bravo.
- And finally room service brownies and ice cream.
- Tom said it was the best birthday ever.

That last line was the greatest of all great things.

RETURN FROM INDY – DECMEBER 28, 2018:

- Hit the breakfast buffet at the Embassy Suites.
- Then we drove to Edinburgh.
- We spent a little time at the outlet malls and then we found the biggest antique mall we've ever seen: The Exit 76 Antique Mall
 (http://www.exit76antiques.com/)
- They have over 5,000,000 items.
- We barely put a dent into that number.
- Tom can't wait to come back during Spring Break.
- We had a late lunch at Cracker Barrel then headed home.

    We spent two more days in Indy over spring break. It took us two trips to get through the entire Exit 76 Antiques Mall. The place is huge. (More on that later)

BETH'S BIRTHDAY AT CAMP - SEPTEMBER 17, 2016

- Got to spend the day at our Boy Scout camp with Beth.
- And also my troop.
- 19,382 steps.
- Beth got to go home and sleep in the comfortable bed.

- I'm sleeping in a tent.
- But it is her birthday...
- And it's a perfect night for sleeping in a tent.

MY BIRTHDAY – NOVEMBER 1, 2017

- I got around 300 happy birthday wishes from Facebook friends. Thanks! You're all the greatest!
- Beth's knee surgery went better than expected.
- I started reading a new book on my list of 100 and it's a good one: How Will You Measure Your Life? By Clayton Christensen.
- Also got my next audio book (from the list of 100): Zero to One by Peter Thiel.
- Went on a nice run in the warm weather.
- Got all kinds of cool presents from the family: A light weight golf bag (from Beth), a CD (from Kenny), a handmade KCup variety pack (from Joe) and a Jungle Jim's dark chocolate bar (From Tom).
- And Amazon gift cards!

One of the cool things about Facebook is all the birthday wishes. Some from friends from grade school. Some from college friends. Some from new friends. Some from Toastmasters.

My goal on all of my birthday wishes is to respond with "Thank you". If someone took the time to wish me a happy birthday I can take the time to say thanks. (Even if it us using copy/paste).

OUR WEDDING ANNIVERSARY! - OCTOBER 27, 2018

- Beth and I went to the Y in the morning.
- Beth, Joe, Tommy, Beth's sister Paige and Beth's parents celebrated our 28th anniversary at Red Lobster.
- I had fresh caught Mahi Mahi.
- And Beth shared some shrimp with me!
- After dinner stop at the Goodwill store.
- Beth found a really cool crystal angel.
- And I found a football game I couldn't live without.

Every year we have a great anniversary celebration.

Even if we don't go all the way to Dunn River Falls, Jamaica like we did on our honeymoon!

THANKSGIVING – NOVEMBER 24, 2016

- Turkey, turkey and more turkey.
- Potatoes, corn, mixed veggies, stuffing and more.
- And Beth Barth's pumpkin pie - which I believe is now my favorite pie. I used to think blueberry or peach, but my wife's pumpkin pie is awesome!
- Found out that my sister in law's guide dog will give a kiss on your mouth if you're trying to take a nap. That in itself is NOT a great thing (in fact it's a gross thing), but having that knowledge for the future is a great thing.
- But before the feast / family / football party... we participated in the Williamsburg Hunger walk 5K.
- The community filled a 15-person van with food for the local food pantry.

THANKSGIVING - NOVEMBER 23, 2017

- Woke up and had LL Bean maple coffee with breakfast.
- Beth and I went to the Williamsburg Hunger Walk.
- So did Jesse. He was a good boy on the walk.
- My Fitbit gave me extra credit for having a dog pulling on my arm - so Jesse was actually a very good boy.
- I've never had this happen before: My 10,000th step was actually a sneeze. Meanwhile...
- Beth made crock pot mac and cheese and pumpkin pies so the house smelled awesome.
- We went to Paige's house for lunch.
- And dinner.

We have Thanksgiving down to a science. Beth's sister hosts the dinner. This works because she has the biggest TV for football watching. Beth's mom makes the turkey next door.

We actually have a Thanksgiving Day lunch. Then we take naps and/or watch football. Meanwhile, Beth, her mom, sisters and nieces divide up who will get what from the individual Christmas lists. After lunch, football, naps and card games, we go back for seconds on the turkey.

But before the feast we start with the Williamsburg Hunger Walk. We donate food then walk on the hike/bike trail for 5 kilometers. For added fun we take our black lab Jesse on the walk and play "Guess when he's going to poop". The usual answer is "right on the street", even though the 5K walk is 4.9 miles on the trail and only 0.1 on a street.

BLACK FRIDAY - NOVEMBER 25, 2016

- Had leftover dinner at my in laws. Turkey was just as good as the day

before. Beth's pumpkin pie was even better.
- Huge Nerf war with Joe, Kenny and Tom. Nerf darts were scattered across three floors of the house. Ambushes, backstabbing, laughter.
- Added a bigger nerf gun to my Christmas list. Oh wait - that was supposed to be a secret. Don't tell my sons.
- Went to Kohl's late - still found a bunch of great stuff including some more Christmas gifts.

    This is our standard Black Friday strategy. We sleep in, and shop online, working from the gift lists provided on Thanksgiving Day. After sleeping in we have plenty of energy for a Nerf Dart war. And playing with dogs.

As I like to call it - Black Lab Friday.

THANKSGIVING SATURDAY – NOVEMBER 26, 2016

- Beth, Tom and I went to the Y. Beth did a mile on the indoor track, Tom did the elliptical and I lifted weights.
- I got the Christmas tree up.
- And the house lights. Okay... it's one of those put the laser light generator in the yard and shine the lights on the house... but it works!

GREAT FAMILY TRADITIONS

- Kenny showed me his latest musical composition - it's great.
- Beth and I hit Meijer, got more Christmas shopping done. I don't want to jinx it, but we are way ahead of schedule this year...
- We had the third of four dinners with Beth's family.

The food, wine and laughter are why this is one of my favorite times of the year. Depending on how ravenous we were on Thursday and Friday we may or may not have turkey left on Saturday.

Frequently we have turkey noodle soup. I don't get sick of turkey. I can eat it every day for a long time. I'm not sure how long of a time, because we always run out of turkey before I get tired of it.

I'll admit - I'm addicted to Thanksgiving leftovers. And I don't think I could quit cold turkey #dadjoke.

CHRISTMAS WALK – DECEMBER 2, 2016

- We had dinner at the Methodist church. Turkey or ham (Beth and I had turkey, Tommy had a little of each), dressing, mashed potatoes, etc.
- Kenny had spaghetti from the Presbyterian church but brought it over and ate with us. (Kenny didn't switch teams, but they do make some good spaghetti...)
- Most of the local businesses were open and had some cool displays. We stopped at...
- The library, where I found a book at the used book sale.
- The Village Barber shop. Pete had a really cool bears playing Christmas music on a xylophone toy.
- Wrinkles Antiques where Tommy got a stocking.
- Herbst Insurance Agency where they had some really cool electric trains.
- Speaking of electric trains, I learned that it's not a good idea to play with trains at dinner if you're having decaf and wearing light jeans. The great thing is they are lined jeans, so the coffee didn't feel that hot when it made it to my leg.
- The Brownies were giving away brownies for donations as a fund raiser (pretty clever when you think about it - if Tiger Cub Scouts were giving away tigers that wouldn't be nearly as well received).
-With all that walking, both Beth and I were over 10,000 steps. I was

holding hands with Beth and felt her Fitbit go off at 10,000 steps.

The Christmas Walk is a holiday tradition in our town. The stores and businesses are open late. They have hot cider or hot chocolate available – sometimes with cookies. The two largest churches in town serve dinner (Methodists serve turkey, Presbyterians serve spaghetti). The fire department has fire truck rides through town.

Traditionally this festival happens the first Friday evening in December. Not traditionally, but usually, it's the coldest Friday in December. I don't know why it works out that way. But I remember sitting in the back of the fire truck freezing when our boys were younger.

This year it was actually not terribly cold. But I had lined jeans on just in case. And (as pointed out above) I needed them when I spilled coffee.

CHRISTMAS SHOPPING DAY – DECEMBER 9, 2017

- It was the annual day of vacation / Christmas shopping with Beth.
- We hit Kohl's, Toys R Us, Bath and Body Works, JC Penney, Sears, Kroger and Sam's Club.
- Then we came home and got a bunch of stuff on Amazon.
- While we were out shopping we had lunch at Panera.
- I had a free birthday cookie on my Panera card so we split that for dessert.
- We got home in time to get Tommy Barth off the bus and give him a ride back the (frozen) driveway.
- We had a great fire in the fireplace.
- Banana milkshakes for our bedtime snack.

Every year Beth and I take a day of vacation and set out with the goal of completing our Christmas shopping. With online shopping this goal has gotten easier over the years. In fact, most of the day is centered around finding items for stockings.

We start at Bath and Body Works. Beth has all of her coupons and gift cards ready to go. We get enough items to fill stockings (well, the part that won't have candy or other trinkets anyway). Then I calculate how much shower gel / shampoo I'm going to need over the next year, and buy it all right then. We hit Kohl's (ornaments) and one or two other stores. We might hit Ollie's Outlet or Target.

After our shopping we go someplace to enjoy lunch together. It's usually Panera or Bob Evans. We return home and hide anything we have bought for the kids.

The best part of the day is unplugging from the inevitable holiday rat race and spending some time together.

THE GREAT ORNAMENT DRAFT – DECEMBER 23, 2016

- Got a load of gravel down on the driveway (with help from Kenny).
- Got the second load of gravel ready to go for today.
- Walked outside.
- Dinner (by the bite) at my sister in law's.
- Great wine service from my niece Sarah.
- The ornament draft was a huge success.
- Lots of laughs with family.

In addition to our normal Christmas traditions, our in-laws said we could each pick one ornament from the tree. I was drafting fifth. It was the ultimate Christmas Gift. I got to be a General Manager!

I traded my pick to my niece Sarah in exchange for her pick (sixth overall) and wine delivery all holiday. I offered Tom that pick for his pick (#11) and one free hour of labor.

Tom didn't see a franchise ornament at six, so the trade didn't happen.

THE GREAT DALMUTI – DECEMBER 24, 2016:

- First thing in the morning we had the "Brothers gift exchange". This is a family tradition, dating back to the time when we first had three brothers (so maybe 15 years). The logic is this: The boys can't wait to open a gift,

so they each open two (one from each of their two brothers) on Christmas Eve Day.
- Family Christmas Eve Dinner. We filled the grill with all kinds of good food, then we emptied it (for the most part anyway). This is a new tradition. We grill on Christmas Eve (and have done it since 2015).
- Huge family game of The Great Dalmuti.
- Dalmutis were named, then defeated. Tiaras were worn, pictures were taken and posted on Facebook.
- In other words, we had a blast.
- Merry Christmas! May Great Things happen to you on this Christmas Eve and on Christmas Day as well!

Note that several skewers are on the grill where the handles would melt and/or fall off if I didn't notice them. I wound up throwing out several skewers.

FAMILY CHRISTMAS - DECEMBER 25, 2016:

- Started out the day having a bowl of cereal with Beth.
- Well, we each had a bowl of cereal – we didn't split one. For one thing, she doesn't like Frosted Mini Wheats.
- Opened gifts at home with the family.
- Went to my in-laws, opened stockings and had second breakfast.
- Went to church for Christmas service.
- While doing announcements I searched for the word "foyer" but came up with "waiting room" - which is at least funny.

- Came back to my in-laws and opened gifts.
- Came home and got a quick nap
- Then we played cards. The game was one I got for Christmas: One Night Ultimate Werewolf. It comes with an app - too much fun!
- We took a dinner break
- Turkey, dressing, basically a Thanksgiving do-over.
- Then more One Night Ultimate Werewolf.
- We're probably going to play it again tomorrow.

One of my 2016 Christmas gifts was the card game "One Night Ultimate Werewolf".

After lunch we said "Let's play cards!" Normally this means "The Great Dalmuti" but we decided to try something different.

We opened Ultimate Werewolf and gave it a try. The game involves lying and deception, and a lot of laughter. We were hooked. We played the rest of the day on Christmas, and then started up again on the 26th.

FAMILY CHRISTMAS - DECEMBER 25, 2017

- An awesome family Christmas.
- Gifts were exchanged.
- Lots of food was consumed.
- And some wine, egg nog and more.
- We played my new game - One Night Ultimate Alien.
- I managed a Christmas nap.

It was a day where we celebrated our family, celebrated how blessed we are - now and forever.

3 | THE ANNUAL FAMILY VACATION

The annual late May or early June trip to Charleston, South Carolina is a great long-standing family tradition. The first time Beth and I went with Beth's family was the summer of 1992. We have been back almost every year since. The vacation is a tradition. And we have traditions within the tradition:

- We rent a house on Isle of Palms for a week.
- We take off the day before our rental starts and drive to Charlotte.
- We stop for dinner at Pirate's Landing Seafood Restaurant in Elkin North Carolina. (http://www.pirateslanding-nc.com/)
- We stay at an Embassy Suites in Charlotte. (The game is to get there in time for Happy Hour. We always win the game).

And that's just the trip to get there!

What follows is some of the greatest of great things from our annual Charleston vacation.

EMBARRASSING VACATION EVENTS – JUNE 5, 2017:

- Had tacos that Beth's sister and mom made for dinner.
- No kale on the tacos.
- Joe volunteered to write the prior two lines for me.

- We compared notes of who had done the most embarrassing thing on vacation so far, and I was only in 3rd place.
- And 4th.
- But the winning "embarrassing vacation" story that my father in law told made me laugh until I cried.
- As did a few good puns from Joe - not the least of which was him taking out four coffee mugs, putting them on the table and saying "It's muggy in here..."
- And then there was the pun he made about "flash floods"... But I digress...
- Kenny and Joe got to play with Chase (Paige's guide dog) at the pool.
- Bedtime snack of leftover chips and hummus (from room service last night).

The winning entry from the most embarrassing thing on vacation: My father in law took my sister in law and her guide dog out to poop after dinner (to be clear – we're talking about the guide dog pooping. My sister in law is for the most part toilet trained.)

After the dog did his business my father in law picked it up, bagged it, and threw it in what he thought was a dumpster.

It turned out the dumpster was in fact a motorcycle trailer.

CHARLESTON TRADITIONS - JUNE 6, 2016:

- We toured Fort Moultrie and the beach in the morning... before the all day rain hit.
- Once the rain hit we went to the antique malls.
- I found a Christmas stein at one of the malls.
- Beth found a really cool carving.
- Joe and Tom found cool stuff too.
- Dinner at Sticky Fingers
- I managed to eat fairly healthy (pulled chicken, light on the sauce, sweet potato casserole and corn on the cob).
- We told clean limericks (both of them) and laughed.
- Then we had some wine, pretzels, ice cream etc. for a bed time snack.

One of our favorite family traditions is a tour of Fort Moultrie on

Sullivan's Island. We started the tradition the first time we stayed on Sullivan's Island. Since then we have moved to Isle of Palms – so we take the ten minute trip to Fort Moultrie every vacation.

Fort Moultrie sits across the harbor from its more famous neighbor, Fort Sumter. The current fort is kept in a similar condition to what it was in World War II. It's neat to walk around, inside and out, and check out the cannons, the underground bunker, powder magazines, etc.

They also have a visitor center with a movie theater. The movie is a 22 minute history of the fort "acted" out by a single actor. The movie itself was done in the 1970s. It's a dated historical movie, if that's possible.

At this point the movie has almost become a Rocky Horror Picture Show experience for the boys and me, because we know the next line by heart.

Charleston has a lot of historical sites to visit. Another good one is Patriot's Point. It has an aircraft carrier: The USS Yorktown. Very cool.

Family on the deck of the Yorktown. Arthur Ravenel bridge in the background.

SAVING STARFISH – JUNE 7, 2017:

- Beth and Tom and I walked on the beach.
- Tom saved a starfish that had washed up on the beach. When he got it back to the ocean it was stuck to him. I told him "It's laying eggs - they'll enter your system, and eventually hatch out in your digestive system... So we'll need a net to catch them..."
- He laughed, but didn't believe me. Guess I'll save that one for grandkids some day.
- We moved down the beach, and found a bunch of starfish that had washed up
- We threw them back too. About 40 in total.

There have been two times on our vacations when the tide washed in a group of sea creatures. One time was after a storm in 1997. The beach was littered with dead sand dollars. My niece ran ahead of us and collected most of them. This time it was starfish, and they were still alive. Tom and I took turns throwing them (gently) back into the ocean.

It reminded me of the old story, told by Zig Ziglar and others, of the grandpa and grandson walking down the beach. The grandpa was throwing live sand dollars back in the ocean (I'm guessing he got there earlier than we did on that day in 1997). The grandson said "There are 1000s of sand dollars on this beach. What difference can it make to throw some back?" The grandpa picked one up and said "To this one – it makes all the difference in the world."

THE ANNUAL KOHL'S TRIP – JUNE 8, 2016:

- We hiked around Charles Towne Landing.
- Which was part of how I got 16,000 steps.
- Saw bison, turkeys and a bear.
- Got to walk through a re-creation of a 1700s cargo ship.
- Got to walk on the beach before...
- We did our annual vacation Kohl's trip... spent about $60 for a bunch of stuff... We allegedly saved over $400. I don't know that I believe that, but we did get some good bargains.

Several years ago Beth and I earned $80 in Kohl's cash. We ran out of time to get back to Kohl's before vacation, and the cash was going to expire while we were in South Carolina. I looked up Kohl's near Charleston and there was one within five miles of our vacation rental.

I asked Beth if we could go hit Kohl's while we were on vacation. She said "Let me ask my parents if they want to do that." They were all in on that idea. We found all kinds of great items. Items we couldn't get in Ohio.

We've gone back every year since.

WALKING ON THE BEACH AND COLLECTING SHELLS – JUNE 9, 2016

- Two more walks on the beach with Beth.
- I found some pieces of clam shells – I love how they are smooth on the inside.
- Another dip in the pool after the beach.
- Took an outdoor shower after the pool - the outdoor shower has two shower heads.
- Experienced the ultimate #firstworldproblem when the showers ran low on hot water and I had to finish with only one shower head.
- Spent the evening with my niece Sarah and her husband Victor. Opened some wine and ice cream, and had some great conversation.

I keep a smooth shell piece in my pocket. Every time I feel that shell. It creates the spark of gratitude in me. I remember walks on the beach with Beth. And I look forward to our next vacation in South Carolina.

CHARLESTON RIVER DOGS – JUNE 10, 2017

- We had lunch at Acme Lowcountry Kitchen. I had a shrimp and crab omelet that was incredible.
- After lunch walk on the beach with Beth.
- Charleston RiverDogs doubleheader with my father in law and my boys

Kenny, Joe and Tommy.
- We didn't make any wrong turns on the way home.
- I realized we've been doing Riverdogs games since 2001 (when we first saw future major leaguer Rocco Baldelli).
- So it's about time I managed the no wrong turns trick.

If you ever find yourself in Charleston, South Carolina in the summer, take in a RiverDogs game. You can enjoy seeing future (and in the case of the coaches former) major leaguers. You can find dollar beers and all kinds of different foods.

You might see co-owner Bill Murray (I met him once). If you go – avoid the setting sun and sit on the first base side.

DO SOMETHING NEW – JUNE 11, 2016

- Grilled sliders for dinner.
- Tom and I took a quick ride to the beach to get a small bag of sand for one of Tom's projects.
- Kenny, Joe and I went back to the pawn shop. Joe got a really nice Fender Telecaster, and Kenny got a pedal that will allow him to play at church without bringing his amplifier.

THE ANNUAL FAMILY VACATION

- Sarah and I got a good laugh when Siri tried to understand "Hockstock Road". (The family nature of this post prevents me from listing what Siri thought the name was... But use your imagination).

We have been coming to the Charleston area on vacation since 1993. Kenny took his first steps on vacation in Charleston. We have all kinds of wonderful memories. After that large number of years it would be easy to get in a routine all the time. And we do have our favorite things, but every year we make sure we do at least one new thing (new activity, new restaurant, new tour).

New activities have included riding jet skis, doing an after dark ghost tour, multiple new restaurants and visiting a birds of prey sanctuary. The pawn shops were one of the new things in 2016.

Doing new things keeps you young.

BLACK FEDORA THEATRE – JUNE 2, 2018

- Walk on the beach followed by our annual trip to downtown Charleston. We shopped at the Straw Market, walked to the pineapple fountain and finished the evening at The Black Fedora Comedy Mystery Theatre and Shoppe.
- We got to watch how "10% rain" (the forecast) can flood Market Street
- from underneath an awning.
- And we got to see how quickly a business can deploy sandbags...
- And we got to see palmetto bugs trying to escape the sewer grate when it flooded. (I guess that was a grate thing).
- Back to the theatre. I got to play a redneck. And Tommy Barth got to play a maid's assistant. And Beth's dad wound up stealing the show.
- Bottom line - we laughed ourselves silly. It was awesome.

Every year we do something new in Charleston. In 2018 our new activity was The Black Fedora Comedy Mystery Theatre and Shoppe. It's now on our must do list. The entire room is the stage: Four main actors do most of the heavy lifting, but audience members are also given parts. And that's where it gets funny.

We went back in 2019 and Tommy played Chewbacca. I have never heard a better Chewbacca (now that the original Chewbacca is dead. Too soon?).

Nothing against the Charleston Riverdogs games, but after our 2019 trip my father in law said "I enjoyed this more than the game." He wasn't wrong.

GRILL FIX – JUNE 9, 2017

- Grilled skewers for dinner.

Grilled skewers are one of our favorite recipes. Especially when we're on vacation and get fresh caught shrimp.

One time it looked like the grilled dinner might not happen: I turned on the grill, and it wouldn't get hot enough. Plenty of propane, but it just wouldn't warm up.

I googled the symptoms. It said "You probably tripped the regulator. Turn off the burners, but leave the propane on to equalize pressure on both sides of the regulator, then restart. Worked like a charm. And we had grilled skewers within 10 minutes.

FUN ON THE LAST DAY OF VACATION – JUNE 12, 2016:

- One final walk on the beach with Beth.
- And one final dinner.
- And one final chance to annoy our children by dressing alike.

THE ANNUAL FAMILY VACATION

4 | DAY TRIPS

When the kids were younger and all in the same school they had the same spring break. That meant a spring vacation to some place warm (normally). Gatlinburg, Orlando and Washington DC were our favorite destinations.

Now that the kids are older we have separate spring breaks. We changed our strategy to taking day trips. The Cincinnati Zoo, Cincinnati Art Museum and Krohn Conservatory are all on our day trip list.

ZOO PICNIC IN THE CAR – MARCH 27, 2017

- Beth, Tommy and I went to the zoo.
- We had our annual picnic lunch in the car.
- We got to see the hippos, but not the baby Fiona.
- But we did get to see some baby tigers.
- I got to see camels without being spit on.
- We got to touch two different snakes (But I'm still not sure they sell snakes at the zoo... for those of you who saw my earlier post of the school note.)

A word of explanation: Earlier in March Tom got to go to the zoo as part of a school field trip. We received a note that students would be given some time if they wanted to "buy a snake". I'm pretty sure they meant snack.

That didn't stop me from posting it on Facebook.

One more note: I've never had a camel spit at me. But I've heard they can.

ART MUSEUM AND MORE - MARCH 28, 2018

- Beth, Tommy and I went to the Krohn Conservatory to see the Krohn Conservatory Butterflies of Madagascar.
- I had one land on my back and crawl up on my head, but it took off just before I could get a picture. - After that we went to the Cincinnati Art Museum.
- Where we had lunch.
- And checked out the art.
- My father in law stopped by with a wine delivery.
- We opened a couple of Kasteel Winters while he was here.
- Beth made spaghetti for dinner.
- I took a quick after dinner nap.
- Then I swam at the Y.

The cafe at the Cincinnati Art Museum has great food. Plenty of healthy options as well. I generally order something like a beet salad, then give Beth a sad face after I finish. She then gives me part of her sandwich.

Hey if it works for the dogs, it can work for me too.

OHIO STATE FAIR - JULY 29, 2016

- Beth, Tom and I went to the Ohio State Fair.
- We had Thanksgiving lunch for dinner at the Ohio food building.
- I bought a piece of the Berlin wall.
- Tom got to ride a camel. No spitting incidents.
- I got restocked on maple syrup.
- We got some cool stuff at the Commercial Building.
- We got to walk through one of those tiny houses that I always see on the Internet. (It didn't take long).

Every year I take a day of vacation and the family goes to the state fair. The Ohio State Fair is one of the largest in the country. We have a route through the fair that works pretty well. It lands us at the Ohio food building for lunch, and then back at the Ohio food building for milkshakes later in the day.

If you go to the Ohio State Fair here's a life hack: The line for milkshakes at the Butter Cow building is insane. The exact same milkshakes are available at the Ohio Food Building. With a much shorter line.

From a prior trip to the state fair. I stood a safe distance from the camel

5 | SHOPPING – KOHL'S AND MORE

We love to shop. Our department store of choice is Kohl's. There are lots of reasons why we shop there, but if I had to choose one, it would be the "savings game".

If you shop at Kohl's, you occasionally get an additional 30% off savings sticker. You even get an extra 30% off on clearance items. If something is 80% or 90% off you get that plus an additional 30%. (Note: That doesn't mean they pay you to take the item. It means that the $40 Jerry Garcia tie that was marked down to $4.00 will now cost you $2.80).

There are also times when you get $10 Kohl's cash for every $50 in purchases.

Then there are those glorious times when you get both.

It becomes a game. A game we play pretty well.

WE SAVED HOW MUCH? – MARCH 18, 2016:

- Beth and I hit the sales at Kohl's, and "saved" $1159.
- We found Levis for all the kids.
- And sweaters
- And coats.
- And jeans for me.

- And cool gifts for our Christmas in July party.

I don't believe that we saved $1159 at Kohl's. For one thing, I don't pay full price on anything at Kohl's. But it was fun to hear our checkout lady turn to the other checkout lady and say "WOW! Check out how much they saved!"

It was even more fun when we came back a couple of months later and she said...

"I RECOGNIZE YOU - YOU'RE THE BARGAIN HUNTERS."

THE KOHL'S CASH VORTEX - MARCH 30, 2017:

- Ran outside. It's starting to look a lot like spring.
- Beth, Tommy and I went to Kohl's to use our Kohl's cash.
- We wound up earning more Kohl's cash.
- Jesse is learning his commands from puppy class.
- Really good project call. I'm fortunate to work with a lot of helpful and collaborative people across the company.
- Finished up the day with an episode of "The Librarians" with Beth and Tommy.

Every so often we get caught in what I like to call the "Kohl's Cash Vortex."

It starts innocently enough. We go to Kohl's, hit the clearance racks, get some good stuff, and some Kohl's cash.

Then we go back to spend the Kohl's cash, and wind up earning more Kohl's cash. So we have to go back again.

In this case, we didn't get through all the clearance racks the first time, so we went back with our cash, went through more clearance stuff, spent our Kohl's cash, spent some real money and earned more cash. (We had an additional 20% off - that always helps).

Then just when I thought we could escape, Kohl's they sent us an additional 30% off coupon. So I pulled out my "Things I will get the next time we have 30% off at Kohl's list" (Yeah, that's what I call it). I got work shoes (Sketchers) and running shoes (Asics). And a few other things.

This of course meant we earned more Kohl's cash.

Eventually we broke the cycle. This involves going in, and buying k-cups with the Kohl's cash.

GETTING OUT OF THE VORTEX - DECEMBER 26, 2017

- The guys (Phil, Kenny, Joe and Tommy, plus Sarah's husband Victor and Beth's dad Kenny) went to Cici's Pizza and Jungle Jim's.
- 30 minutes swimming earlier in the day to help offset the Christmas diet.
- Beth's parents came over for leftovers for dinner.
- Including Beth's incredible pumpkin pie.
- After dinner Kohl's date with Beth. Not much Christmas clearance stuff left, but we did find enough to use our Kohl's cash, and (most importantly) not earn any more Kohl's cash. #outofthevortex

BIG SHOE SCORE AT KOHL'S - NOVEMBER 25, 2017

- Three trips to Kohl's in a row (including one in Memphis) I looked for Asics shoes and came away empty.
- Tonight I walk to the shoe department at Kohl's. I take the obligatory glance at the clearance rack. - I see four pairs of Asics.
- I figure there's no way they'll be in my size (ten).
- I was wrong. Three out of four times!
- Bonus: Since it was Black Friday I got $15 cash back on every $50 I spent.

HOW TO USE KOHL'S CASH – DECEMBER 2, 2016

- We went to Sam's Club and Kohl's.
- At Kohl's we spent our Kohl's cash, and about six dollars more. Five bucks of that was Tom, so we actually wound up getting clothes, candles and k-cups for a buck.
- Went up to the Old Firehouse Brewery with Kenny, Joe and Tommy. Beers and orange sodas. I swear their orange soda is the best stuff ever.
- Well, it wasn't as good as the 4 beer flight I had, but it was good.

If I don't have the time (or inclination) I buy k-cups with my Kohl's cash. Or jockey t-shirts. Basically anything where I can't get the additional 20 to 30% off. If I have an extra 30% off, anything that costs $10 in Kohl's cash would only cost $7 in real money. K-Cups and Jockey T-Shirts cost $10 in either currency.

Kohl's is nice, but there is another even more fun shopping experience for the family: Second hand sales.

This can be hitting an Antique Mall, a Goodwill Store (the Cincinnati Beechmont store is a excellent), a Flea Market like Treasure Aisles or Traders' World (both north of Cincinnati) or the king of all second hand sales: The garage sale!

GARAGE SALE FINDS - SEPTEMBER 11, 2016

- Tom and I worked on his homework on the deck, because...
- The weather was absolutely perfect, and...
- We heard a catbird while we were out there.
- Beth made chili spaghetti for dinner.
- Then we took a walk.
- Over 14,000 steps for the day
- We helped clean up the football field before Upward sports.
- I found a partial pineapple under the visitor's bleachers, which I found both nasty and hilarious.
- On the way home we saw 4 plastic chairs and a director's chair at St.

SHOPPING – KOHL'S AND MORE

Anne's rummage sale. We got em.

One of the highlights of our community garage sale weekend is our local Catholic Church rummage sale. We know it's going to be a winner, because even if we don't find anything in the sale we will buy incredible baked goods. It's probably a good thing they only do this twice a year.

The plastic chairs from this sale got two coats of blue paint. They have been on Beth's parents' pool deck ever since. The director's chair needed a new seat and back after the original broke. All in all not bad for five bucks (total – a dollar per chair).

THRIFT IS IN THE GENES - DECEMBER 15, 2017

- Talked with mom on the phone.
- We compared L L Bean bargains.
- She has a pair of lined jeans for $5 (Goodwill).
- I have dress shirts for $1 (church rummage sale).
- We also like LL Bean's regular store and catalog items but there's something about getting the big bargain...
- Beth and I took the day off.
- We hit Kohl's (extra 30%!!!), Bath and Body Works, Sam's Club and Aldi (they had 99 cent pineapples)
- And we had lunch at Panera.
- We brought a cookie home for Tom so he wouldn't be too upset about missing Panera.

Two notes: First - As noted in the title I come by my thrifty shopping honestly. Not just from mom either.

One of my dad's legendary quotes was at a garage sale when he brought up a coat that was marked $10 and asked the lady running the sale...

"WHAT IS THE ABSOLUTE LEAST YOU WILL TAKE FOR THIS COAT?"

(Answer was $4).

Second - This post gives props to my home church - Williamsburg United Methodist Church. I bought four LL Bean wrinkle free cotton dress shirts - they looked brand new and custom fitted - for $1 each.

FAVORITE WORKOUT SHIRTS – MAY 13, 2016

- I planned out the day first thing in the morning
- I realized it would be tight to finish everything on my list.
- Then a 1 1/2 hour meeting got canceled. I got the list done and more.
- As I left work I saw a turtle crossing the road. I stopped the car and relocated it.
- When I got back in the car I found my sunglasses on the floor.
- Installed the shelves in the attic.
- When I ordered the shelves I threw in two $3 t-shirts to get free shipping. They arrived today.
- And they're my favorite t-shirts.

Shipping was $8.95 if the order was less than $50. It was free if the order was over $50. I was a little more than $5 short. So I saved almost $4 by getting the two shirts. And three years later they are still my favorite exercise shirts.

THE BEST WAY TO SHOP AT BEST BUY – JANUARY 27, 2017

- Swimming at the Y with Tommy.
- Beth made chili spaghetti for dinner.
- Kenny, Joe and Tom were all here for dinner.
- After dinner Joe and I went to Kroger and bought some Best Buy gift cards (2x Fuel Points and 3% cash back on AmEx).
- Then we went across the highway and spent the gift cards on Joe's new MacBook Pro.

Joe needed a new MacBook Pro for school. But instead of just going to Best Buy to get it, we bought $1500 worth of Best Buy gift cards at Kroger. This gave us 3000 fuel points (or $1 per gallon off on our next 3 fill ups). At around 11 gallons each that was $33 back.

Add to that the fact that we get 3% cash back on grocery purchases, including gift cards bought at the grocery store. That was another $45 back.

There were also Best Buy reward points in play, but I really don't remember how many. I think it wound up being a free video game.

I do know this: As soon as we pulled out the gift cards the Best Buy salesman said "Oh, you went to Kroger first? Good move." It happens fairly often.

GREAT THINGS HAPPEN EVERY DAY

6 | DAY CAMP

Beth is the Camp Director for our District's Cub Scout Community Day Camp. Five days of outdoor fun with around 150 Cub Scouts and 75 volunteers.

Day Camp week is one of the most "Great Things" weeks in the year. We get up early each day, go to camp, set up and do our jobs. Beth and the other volunteers do all the hard work. I work at the trading post, which means I get to sit in the shade and spend the better part of the day laughing with the health officer - my buddy Jason. (Humor to follow… at least what Jason and I define has humor).

At the end of the day we then go to Beth's mom and dad's or her sister Paige's for dinner and (weather permitting) a swim.

We come home, finish up our work, make lunches for the next day, and repeat the process. It's a lot of fun, and 150 kids get to have a great week at camp that they'll remember for a lifetime.

YOO HOO! – JULY 10, 2016

- Beth and I found 12 12 packs of Yoo Hoo for Day Camp (at Kroger).

Yoo Hoo is the official drink of Day Camp. (For the scouts anyway. Most adults think it tastes like chocolate water). The year after I wrote this I discovered that Wal Mart carries 12 packs of Yoo Hoo and will ship them for free if you buy enough (we always do).

It's very unlikely I will ever get to pose for a picture like this again. I can live with that.

START OF DAY CAMP – JULY 18, 2017

- Smoothie for breakfast.
- For lunch we had pizza from LaRosa's.
- It was free! 11 strikeouts x 4 tickets = 4 free pizzas.
- Picked a bunch more blackberries after day camp.
- Swimming after that.
- Dinner at Kenny and Joyce's.

Normally we pack our lunch for day camp. On this day however we had tickets from a recent Reds game where the Reds struck out 11 (or more batters). Each ticket got us a free pizza.

There were times when we weren't so fortunate with the strikeouts. (See also "Miscellaneous Stories - this was the time you almost got free pizza")

BANANA BOATS – JULY 19, 2017

- Smoothie for breakfast (second day in a row).
- Got a half hour walk at camp before it got really hot.
- Got to share "Airplane!" movie quotes with Jason.
- Dinner at Paige's. Enchiladas!
- Picked a lot of blackberries.
- Hit the pool after blackberry picking.
- Had a water balloon broken on my back at camp, which was really quite

refreshing.
- Planned my revenge for the water balloon.
- We made banana boats at camp – banana, chocolate chips and marshmallows wrapped in foil and cooked in the fire pit.
- I tried something new – Banana and Twizzlers wrapped in foil and cooked in the fire pit.
- It was delicious... and by that I mean disgusting. Twizzlers don't melt well at all.

Banana Boats Recipe:
- Take a banana and cut a ¾ inch wide slice from top to bottom. Do NOT fully remove that part of the peel.
- Pull back the peel, and scoop out some of the banana inside with a spoon (and go ahead and eat it).
- Replace the banana you scooped out with chocolate chips and miniature marshmallows.
- Put the peel back and wrap the banana in foil.
- Put the banana on the coals in the fire pit (this is done by my father in law for the scouts, but you can do it all by yourself).
- After a few minutes, take the banana out of the fire pit, let it cool enough to remove the foil, and eat it with a spoon.

GETTING FITBIT STEPS THE EASY WAY (AKA CHEATING) – JULY 20, 2017

- We got to see a bloodhound and police drug dog in action at camp. (It was a demo...). Very cool dogs.
- My mother in law made homemade pizza and blackberry dumplings for dinner.
- Swimming pool after blackberry picking.
- My friend Bill is getting all kinds of steps at camp and winning the Fitbit challenge.
- But I may have come up with a way to compete.

    The idea was to set up the kids Geotrax train, put the Fitbit in a car, and run the train while resting in the hammock. This was based on a similar idea that the boys had to get activity points in a Pokemon game (put the iPhone on the train). The iPhone was far too heavy and the train tipped over.

The Fitbit was better, but the steps weren't that great. I would have needed to run it all night. But it does show how innovation happens. Start with one idea, and build on it. (Did I just compare trying to cheat in a race to innovation? Wow.)

DAY CAMP HUMOR (AT LEAST WE THOUGHT IT WAS FUNNY) – JULY 21, 2017

- We had another great day at Day Camp.
- Spaghetti and meatballs from Paige for dinner. Delicious.
- Homemade milkshakes or (in my case) Apple Pie ice cream for dinner.
- 10,000 steps.
- A great idea for day camp: have the health officer take the cart around and yell "Bring out your dead!"

(Idea was vetoed)

- Great thing I learned today: kids who cut themselves while whittling don't particularly enjoy my Julia Child SNL impression.

- Beth told the kids working at hospitality that they needed to take a drink of water every time Jason or I said something stupid and/or obnoxious. She said that would keep them hydrated.
- We're now worried about water poisoning.

In subsequent years we upped our humor game (in our opinion only). We added a large Bluetooth speaker. (This was also used for the Day Camp Dance Party – see picture). When kids were brought to the medical tent we would play a variety of songs ("Stayin Alive" "Another One Bites the Dust" "Dr. Feelgood" and "Dead or Alive" were among the favorites.)

We will... we will... rock you!

BISCUITS ON A STICK – JULY 22, 2017

- Conclusion to a very successful day camp!
- Smoothie for breakfast.
- Low sodium / low fat Swiss cheese sandwich for lunch.
- Low fat burgers for dinner.
- 13,000 steps.
- Huge thunderstorm, which was great because it watered my blackberries.
- The fire trucks visited day camp.

    We finish every day camp with a visit from the fire department. They spray water in the air, and the scouts run around and get soaked. We have, in the past, had squirt gun wars, but some people took them too seriously. So we stopped doing that. Even after I apologized.

Biscuits on a Stick Recipe:

- Open a can of Pillsbury biscuits.
- Pull out one biscuit. Roll it into a snake shape, then wrap it around a foil covered stick. (If you're afraid of snakes you can roll in into a worm shape).
- Put it over the fire and rotate it until it turns yellow to brown, depending on how dark you like it.
- Brush melted butter on the biscuit, then pour cinnamon and sugar on top.

7 | THE WORLD CHAMPIONSHIP OF PUBLIC SPEAKING

Maybe you've heard it before: The number one fear of people is public speaking. Number two is death.

You've also likely heard the joke that goes with it: That means the average person would rather be in the casket than delivering the eulogy.

I'm not afraid of Public Speaking. I never have been. Note: I'm not fearless in general. Snakes scare the crap out of me. Not a huge fan of heights either. Or hotels with slow wifi. Or kale. Oh yeah, and death.

But I digress.

Public speaking has never been a fear. There was, however, a time when I should have been afraid to speak in public. How do I put this nicely? I sucked at it.

After getting some feedback ("You should be afraid to speak in public." "Or private." "You suck.") I joined Toastmasters.

Toastmasters International (www.toastmasters.org) is an organization dedicated to helping people improve their communication and leadership skills. Every year Toastmasters has a speech contest that starts in February (more or less) and ends in August. Approximately 20,000 Toastmasters compete through as many as six levels with one person left at the end: The World Champion of Public Speaking.

I started competing in 2001.

In 2011 I made it to the finals of the World Championship of Public Speaking, where I lost fairly convincingly. Still, I got to speak in the finals in front of 2000 people in Las Vegas. Not bad.

In 2015 I made it back to the semi-finals (again in Las Vegas) but, as already noted, never made it to Las Vegas thanks to a "small" heart attack.

In 2018 I started on another journey. The story of that journey follows. But before we get started, I need to add one more thing: The number one fear of people is not public speaking. It's making an ass of themselves. It's just that public speaking (without Toastmasters) is a good way to do that. Ask me how I know…

CREATING A SPEECH ON THE FLY – JULY 12, 2017:

- I attended a Toastmasters meeting with what will be my second club.
- They didn't have any speakers signed up.
- So I signed up quickly.
- I told the story of my weekend (Thanks to the things Michael Davis has taught me I was able to put it together on the fly).
- I gave the speech. You would think that I could finish in under 7 minutes since I just came up with it…
- Well, close. 7:08.
- As always, I recorded it.
- I'm fairly certain I now have the guts of my 2018 contest speech.

And in fact I did have the guts of my contest speech. I told the story of our trip to Mammoth Cave. Of course when a trip involves my flight home being delayed by a day, then me getting stung in the eye by a wasp, then me hitting a car in a parking lot, then us seeing a car going sideways in the median of the highway… that makes an easy speech.

MY LAST TOASTMASTERS SPEECH CONTEST, MAYBE – JANUARY 4, 2018:

- Worked on my 2018 contest speech.
- Said (a while ago) that 2018 would be my last contest.
- Yesterday I found out that the 2020 convention is in Paris.
- Changed my mind about 2018 being my last contest.

Throughout the course of the year I went back and forth on 2018 being my last entry in a Toastmasters speech contest. I would say "This is my last contest" to force myself to do the absolute most I could to prepare for 2018. If it's your last contest, you're more likely to go all out. You might even skip watching a game on TV. Or I would say it when I started to get burnt out by the prep. "I can't take it – this is my last one."

One time I actually said "If I decide to compete after 2018 I will eat kale for a week." But then I would have a breakthrough and decide "Yeah, I might keep competing after all." The final decision was made in August.

WHY I RECORD MY SPEECHES – FEBRUARY 3, 2017:

- Took the puppy on 3 walks.
- He slept really well after that.
- And I got 13,000 steps.
- Plus a lot of speech practice.
- I forgot a line when I was practicing my speech, so I put it in later (Like I would have done in the actual contest).
- And I realized that's where the line belonged the whole time. It was cleaner and it saved me 5 words.

This is one reason I record my speeches. When I drift away from the script there's a (small) chance that I will say something better than originally written. In fact, there are times when I'm writing a speech that I can't figure out parts of the message. So my notes just say "Talk about what you learned".

I record what I say to the audience, and that gives me a great start for the script of the speech. That said, this wasn't a practice I recorded. It's a little hard to record a speech given while walking the dog. But I did carry my phone. I stopped and recorded the idea.

I read once that the average idea is gone from our head within 30 seconds. If it's not recorded, it's gone. I'm the person who pulls the average down to 30 seconds. If I don't grab it in five seconds, it's gone.

But I got this one on the phone, and I used it in the speech.

AREA SPEECH CONTEST - MARCH 15, 2018

- Won the Toastmasters Area speech contest.
- Also practiced my speech at my BTC club, and got more great feedback!
- Got a pre-contest swim in at the Y.
- And a post-contest lift before I picked up Tommy at the bowling alley.
- And by "lift" I mean 3 machines, one set each, slow lifting (ten seconds per rep), to total exhaustion. (Minimal effective dose, learned from Tim Ferriss' book The Four Hour Body).
- In other words, I was in and out of the Y in 15 minutes (the second time), including time to change.

DIVISION SPEECH CONTEST - APRIL 29, 2018:

- I left our campout to compete in the 2018 Toastmasters Division I Speech Contest.
- I took a selfie with the troop for luck before the contest.
- It worked! I won the Division contest. Next stop: District!

There were a large number of "Great Things" entries that said the same thing "Practiced my speech at a Toastmasters club and got great feedback." Some were in Memphis, most were in the Cincinnati area. All were crucial in making the speech better.

SPEECH CONTEST TRADITIONS – MAY 19, 2018

- Outdoor run before the speech contest to clear my head and get focused.
- Had my customary pre speech meal. A smoothie for breakfast, a protein bar and not much else for lunch.
- And probably a gallon of water throughout the day.
- Drove to the contest venue while listening to Queen (We Will Rock You), Aerosmith, a few specific songs to help me get my head around how to say a certain section of the speech, plus Abba at the end to put me in the right mind set.
- Gave my speech.
- Went to HotHead Burrito with Michael Davis. Mike had his TEDx shirt on and the employees were impressed. I told them that Mike was the speech coach for Anthony Muñoz, and they had a blank look on their faces. Really?
- Went back to the venue and won the contest!
- Came home and ate everything in sight (all healthy, there will be no repeat heart attack this time).
- Finished the day with Beth and Tommy, a glass of raspberry wine, and an episode of Big Bang Theory.

(Note: The District Speech contest is unique in that there is a dinner break between the speech contest and the announcement of results).

The traditions above are repeated before each speech contest. The water is because I want to avoid dry mouth. The meals are to keep me from getting hungry, and also keep me from getting full. I avoid milk and cheese on the last meal because it can cause congestion.

Hothead burrito afterwards was a nice touch. The district contest before that (2015) it was Chipotle with Tom – so I guess there's a post contest burrito tradition going on there.

I still find it hard to believe there are people in the greater Cincinnati area who don't know who Anthony Muñoz is. (He is a hall of fame football player for the Cincinnati Bengals).

"IT FLOWS" – AUGUST 9, 2018

- Got up and ran first thing.
- That meant one of my three Apple watch circles was closed before breakfast.
- Practiced my semi-finals speech. It flows.
- And "It flows" are the exact words I wanted to be able to say about it at this point.
- Talked with Beth about all kinds of stuff - like the great progress Tommy has made on his Eagle project.

The easiest part of a seven minute speech – Toastmasters contest speech or otherwise – is telling the story. I can get roughly 5/7 of a speech finished in one day. In fact, I have done 5/7 of a speech more times than I remember. We all have.

Five minutes out of a seven minute speech are your story. The same stories you tell over lunch. The same stories you tell over a beer. (Well, maybe cleaned up a little).

For a speech contest, the story might need to be modified a little, but it stays mostly unchanged from your lunch version.

It's the remaining 2/7 – the introduction, the conclusion, the occasional bridge between parts of the story, and all of the transitions – that take the majority of the time.

Of the ones listed above, the transitions (at least for me) take the most work. That's why I like to be able to say "It flows". That means the speech goes from introduction, through transitions, through the story, through more transitions and to the conclusion without a hitch.

Once I get there, I can practice the little things to make it even better.

One side note: I see nothing wrong with using PowerPoint, especially in presentation mode, to help with transitions in a keynote. Speaker notes can help. Also putting a question for the audience that guides you through a transition works nicely. Just be ready to go without it if you lose a projector, or have any one of countless other potential technical issues.

INTERESTING SPEECH FEEDBACK: "THAT WAS THE BEST SPEECH I'VE EVER HEARD, BUT I DON'T GET OUT MUCH."

SPEECH PRACTICE – AUGUST 18, 2018

- Practiced my semi-finals speech.
- Practiced my finals speech.
- Practiced my semi-finals speech as fast as possible.
- Practiced my finals speech as fast as possible.
- Practiced my semi-finals speech as slowly as possible.
- Practiced my finals speech as slowly as possible.
- Practiced my semi-finals speech one more time.
- Accidentally said a line that was WAY better than what I had written.
- Stopped and wrote it down.
- Finished practice and opened a Kasteel Rouge.

In my multi-year Toastmasters journey have been coached by several excellent speech coaches.

One of them – Lance Miller (www.lancemillerspeaks.com) recommended the approach above (as fast as possible, as slowly as possible). He also recommended doing it as quietly as possible and as loud as possible.

Repeating the speech in these ways gives the speaker a chance to try something new, which might click. A line that you envisioned being very loud might be more effective if delivered slowly.

Another advantage of this practice method: When you can deliver a speech from memory as slowly as possible, you have it memorized.

THE 2018 WORLD CHAMPIONSHIP OF PUBLIC SPEAKING – AUGUST 21, 2018

- Packed for Chicago.
- Couldn't find my prop for my finals speech. Looked all over the house. Then I took my wife's advice and went up to the church (where I practiced yesterday). Sure enough, it was still laying on the stage.
- Picnic lunch at a rest stop with Beth. We timed it right - the rain was stopped, and it was actually a little cold. For the first time in I don't know how long!
- Shopping at Chicago Premium Outlets. Good thing we drove - we would have paid a fortune in checked luggage on the way home had we flown.
- And I got to take a picture...

THE WORLD CHAMPIONSHIP OF PUBLIC SPEAKING

*I didn't even know this was a real thing
and if I didn't know that…*

- Checked in to Embassy Suites.
- I did one speech practice before bed.

THE 2018 WORLD CHAMPIONSHIP OF PUBLIC SPEAKING – AUGUST 22, 2018

- Wow. Where to start? We drove into Chicago, the traffic wasn't nearly as bad as I thought it might be.
- We got settled in the hotel.
- Then I had the semifinal draw, and got position 10 (of 11). This was followed immediately by the microphone test.
- Then Beth and I had Chicago pizza. I'm still full.
- I talked with all kinds of speaker friends from all over the world including Lance Miller, Darren LaCroix and Jim Key.
- I got to meet, face to face, Russ Dantu and Sarah Khan.
- I practiced my speech with Eric Feinendegen and Jeff Stein.
- I finished the day with some of my in-laws homemade raspberry wine (aka sleeping medicine).

(Need a speaker? Google any of the names above. Or mine. Actually mine first.)

THE 2018 WORLD CHAMPIONSHIP OF PUBLIC SPEAKING – AUGUST 23, 2018

- Gave the best version of my speech yet on the semi-final stage.
- Got a trophy. Second place
– Top 20 in the World.
- And I got to debate the merits of the Cleveland Browns with fellow former Clevelander and honorary niece (and eventual 2018 World Champion of Public Speaking) Ramona J. Smith on stage during the contestant interviews.
- Beth and I took an Uber and enjoyed shopping and dinner in Andersonville.
- After dinner we found out that room service delivered pints of Hagen Das for $5 each.

Even if you don't win it's impossible to be upset when you're sitting with your sweetie eating Hagen Das and drinking homemade raspberry wine.

JOURNEY HOME FROM CHICAGO - AUGUST 24, 2018

- Beth and I had the room service delivered oatmeal (with brown sugar, yellow raisins and pecans) for breakfast.
- We drove to the Field Museum and parked at The Soldier Field parking garage.
- The Bears team shop had the replay of the Browns game on TV.
- There was a long line to get in to the museum, so I went online, found a Groupon, saved $30+ and walked to the head of the will call line (two people deep).
- We explored the mummy exhibit (a little creepy, but interesting), the dinosaur collection (very cool), the gem collection and more.
- And we found cool stuff at the gift shop.
- We drove home, saw the windmill farm again, stopped at the rest areas again, and had almost no traffic delays... until we were within ten miles of home! But we made it through that too.
- Joe and Tommy did a great job of running the house while we were gone.
- I crashed on the couch, slept for an hour, then got up and went to bed - and got a great night's sleep.

As we pulled in to the McDonald's parking on the way home I told Beth "I've made a decision about competing next year" (Because all great decisions are made in a McDonald's parking lot). As long as I can come up with a speech that I really believe in (like this year), and can deliver it with passion (like this year) I will keep competing. (And then we sealed the deal with Egg McMuffins)

So about that whole "This is my last year" thing.... I lied.

And about that whole "I will eat kale for a week if I change my mind" thing... I lied again.

GREAT THINGS HAPPEN EVERY DAY

8 | SEA BASE

In June of 2018 Tom and I (along with three other scouts and one other scout leader) went to Sea Base, a high adventure Boy Scout Camp in the Florida Keys.

Sea Base offers a lot of cool programs. Our program was the "Out Island Adventure". Four days on an island with no electricity, no clocks, no phones. Just fishing, snorkeling and eating. Lots of eating.

I'll admit it now. Four days with no Apple Watch, no iPhone and nothing electric (outside of my CPAP) sounded less like a dream and more like a nightmare. But it turned out to be four of the best days of my life.

That said, I haven't stopped wearing my watch or using my phone since we got back.

SEA BASE TRIP DAY ONE – JUNE 15, 2018

- Got up a 4am to catch an early flight to Fort Lauderdale with Tom and four others.
- Flew to Fort Lauderdale and got our rental van.
- Drove to Homestead and checked in to our Home2Suites room.
- Everyone took a nap.

- Then we went to the Everglades.
- Followed by Cracker Barrel for dinner.
- And a trip to Wal Mart for last minute necessities.

The Everglades were cool. We got to see manatees, baby alligators and tortoises that looked prehistoric.

And of course we saw snakes. I always have to find a snake.

DRIVING TO THE KEYS – JUNE 16, 2018

- Breakfast at Home2Suites. Free and all you can eat!
- Drove from Homestead to the Florida Keys.
- We stopped for lunch on the way.
- Which meant we had fresh seafood!
- Got to Sea Base and checked in.
- Did our swim tests (100 yards in salt water).
- And practiced snorkeling.

Before this trip I hadn't been to the Florida keys in over 20 years. My memory of the keys was a lot of local seafood restaurants right on the water with fresh seafood. I figured things had changed in 20 years. I was delighted to learn that I was wrong.

We had lunch at a Seafood restaurant right on the water. It was a local restaurant. The fish was amazing. As far as I can tell the only thing that changed was the name of the fish: The fish formerly known as Dolphin is now known as Mahi Mahi.

This is a marketing ploy, designed to keep people from asking "Wait – are you serving those cute dolphins?" (Like I asked 20 years before). Mahi Mahi are not particularly cute. More on them in a bit.

There was one other thing that changed over time. The last time I went snorkeling (I was 12 years old) the breathing tube was an open tube. If my head went under, I got a mouth full of salt water. Our breathing tubes now had a valve that kept water out of our mouths. Much better.

ROWING TO THE ISLAND – JUNE 17, 2018

- Rowed five miles out to Big Munson Island. It was a long trip.
- Stopped to go snorkeling. We saw a lion fish (among other things).
- Got to the island and set up camp.
- Cooked dinner (chicken fajitas and fish).

Campsites have tents, a cooking area with picnic table, and propane stove. All food and water is brought in to the camp on a boat (along with my CPAP and battery) and hauled to the site.

DEEP SEA FISHING – JUNE 18, 2018

- Got up and had breakfast.
- Walked down the beach, and through the water to the platform, where the deep sea fishing boats were waiting.
- Got on the boat and headed out to the deep sea.
- Stopped at a school of Yellowtail Groupers. We all caught at least one.
- I caught exactly one.
- Went to deeper waters and trolled for Mahi Mahi.
- We caught two (I caught none). One male, one female. Each of them over two feet long.
- Scouts cleaned the Yellowtail, charter captains cleaned the Mahi Mahi.
- Fish tacos with the Yellowtail and just plain (delicious) fish with the Mahi Mahi.

Okay, maybe I was a little harsh when I said Mahi Mahi are ugly. They actually are kind of a pretty rainbow color, blue and green on top, yellow and orange on their bellies. Female Mahi Mahi are actually pretty. But the males have this big bump on their heads, which moves them from pretty to butt ugly.

(Insert your favorite thick skulled male joke here).

I could share pictures of the Mahi Mahi we caught, but early in the week I learned that my waterproof Go Pro was in fact just a Go Pro.

Whether you consider them pretty or ugly, I know one thing: Mahi Mahi are memorable and delicious. We had leftovers that we shared with other groups who didn't get to fish that day.

SNORKELING – JUNE 19, 2018

- Got up and had breakfast.
- Walked down the beach, and through the water to the platform, where the snorkeling boats were waiting.
- Got on the boat and headed out to Looe Key for snorkeling.
- Tom and I saw all kinds of cool fish and a reef.
- Then we got back into the boat for lunch.
- And I had my first Grape Uncrustable.
- Which was delicious.
- Then we got back in the water to check out a Goliath Grouper that was underneath the boat.
- Easily the biggest fish I've ever seen.

I don't have any pictures of the Goliath Grouper. This is because early on at Sea Base I learned that my waterproof Go Pro camera was in fact just a Go Pro camera. I do have this tip for you (besides "don't buy a 'waterproof' Go Pro"): If you want to see how large a Goliath Grouper really is, go to YouTube and type in "Goliath Grouper".

You will see an option for "Goliath Grouper Eats Shark." In this case, it's a Goliath Grouper eating a four foot long shark.

In. One. Bite.

You can also find "Goliath Grouper eats man". I didn't watch that video.

I also had no idea that either video existed when I got back in the water to check out Mr. Goliath Grouper.

As for the Grape Uncrustable. It turns out that spending a day in the sun and snorkeling makes you very hungry. And as my son Tom says "Hunger is the best sauce. Or at least it's tied with chocolate".

I tried another Uncrustable when I got home (and wasn't quite as hungry). It's certainly not kale, but I feel like I oversold it's deliciousness in this post, and in a few speeches.

OUR OWN PRIVATE BEACH – JUNE 20, 2018

- We took kayaks through the mangrove maze on the island.
- And we hiked around the island.
- We did a service project where we helped put a trail back together.
- The rest of the camp went to night snorkeling.
- Tom and I stayed behind and wound up falling asleep on our air mattresses on the beach.

The service project was a very small part of helping put the island back together. Hurricane Irma did considerable damage to Big Munson Island in September 2017.

As for the night snorkeling: Tom has night blindness. Even with a flashlight he didn't feel comfortable going on a night time snorkel expedition. I was already in the "take it or leave it" camp for nighttime snorkeling. Finding a shark at night didn't sound fun.

Full disclosure: I had a three foot shark swim right past me as I was walking in the shallow part of the ocean. It could have cared less that I was there. (Fortunately there was no Goliath Grouper chasing it).

So Tom and I stayed back at the camp. And everyone else left. Which meant we had our own private island for a couple of hours.

We pulled our air mattresses out of the tent and laid on the beach. We talked for a while, and the next thing you know – we were asleep.

THE LUAU - JUNE 21, 2018

- We rowed the five miles home.
- Within an hour of getting back to the base (and the dorms) a thunderstorm broke loose.
- We had daily threats of storms, but never got one on the island. They

always blew around us. Timing is everything.
- We put our gear away, then got showers and did laundry. Then we had the luau. Every kind of food imaginable.
- After dinner we packed our bags in the car.
- Our flight the next day meant we would wake up around 4am and drive back to Fort Lauderdale.

Queen on the MP3 player (News of the World and A Night at the Opera) and a sunrise before we hit the Florida mainland provided entertainment on the way to the airport. One of the great things now is every time I want to go back to Sea Base, I only need to play Queen. Or maybe look at this picture.

9 | LET'S EAT! AND EXERCISE

I am not an expert on diet and exercise. But this isn't a diet and exercise book. During my great things journey I have picked up a few tips along the way. They are tips that worked for someone who doesn't eat or exercise like Dwayne The Rock Johnson.

I'm making the assumption that anyone reading this book also doesn't eat or exercise like Dwayne The Rock Johnson. I'm on safe ground here, because the only person who eats and exercises like that is in fact Dwayne The Rock Johnson. Therefore I'm making the assumption that Dwayne The Rock Johnson is not reading this book. If I'm wrong and you dear reader are in fact Dwayne The Rock Johnson... well holy crap! How cool is that? I'd be so grateful if you could e-mail me sir: phil@philbarthspeaks

FROSTED MINI WHEATS – JANUARY 3, 2017

- Yesterday Beth and I looked at an article about the best (health wise) cereals. After seeing the "good" ones on the list (Wheat Chex, Total, etc) - I figured out that oatmeal with brown sugar and cinnamon was an even better option. So that's what I had for breakfast.
- And... Frosted Mini Wheats were within 1g of sugar of being on the good list, so guess what I'm having tomorrow?

I love Frosted Mini Wheats. They are a great thing. Sure they have sugar. But they have no sodium, and they have fiber. The article mentioned above looked for cereals that had good fiber, and low (10 grams or less) sugar. Frosted Mini Wheats clear the fiber bar easily, but they have 11 grams of sugar. Close enough. I'll save the gram (aka ¼ teaspoon) of sugar somewhere else.

I've loved Frosted Mini Wheats since I was a kid. And unlike some of the other cereals I loved as a kid (Frosted Flakes, Froot Loops and Super Sugar Crisp) I still love them as an adult. I'm not alone. When I travel I can't help but notice that the Hilton has Frosted Mini Wheats on their breakfast buffet. And there aren't any kids at the 7am during the week Memphis breakfast buffet. I'm not sure if this qualifies as a diet tip or not – but I'm tagging it as such.

ALADDIN'S EATERY – JANUARY 6, 2017

- Had lunch with my friend Chris.
- We discussed Cleveland sports, and life in general. It was great catching up.
- Lunch was at Aladdin's Eatery West Chester, and my Jasmine's favorite with tuna was outstanding.
- I have a piece of leftover grilled tuna for today.
- I didn't get the Shistawook with garlic sauce (that used to be my favorite), which meant I didn't reek of garlic when I got home. (Beth doesn't consider garlic reek a #greatthing)

I first discovered Aladdin's Eatery in Cleveland several years ago. The locals said "If you like Mediterranean food – you have to try this place." It was (and is) delicious.

When you walk in the restaurant and see Danny Ferry (former Cleveland Cavalier, and at the time the GM of the Cavaliers) you figure it's going to be pretty good. I don't think that Danny Ferry eats at lousy restaurants.

Aladdin's is a chain. When I got home I checked out their website, just in case they had a local option. Sure enough, they have one in West Chester. That's an hour from where I live, but only 25 minutes from my office.

I look for excuses to eat there. I generally find one or two a year.

Lunch with my grade school / high school / college / adult friend Chris is a great excuse.

And if you're looking for an entrée with low fat, low sodium, high protein and delicious – Jasmine's favorite with tuna is the way to go.

SWEET POTATOES – JANUARY 19, 2017

- Got to play with the puppy!
- Grilled pork chops and baked sweet potatoes for dinner.
- Speaking of books - good progress on my book. Michael Ireland gave me a great idea for the title.
- We got the new Pinewood Derby track set up. It looks great!

If you aren't a fan of veggies, I have a suggestion: Sweet potatoes. We always get them for under $1 a pound. Sometimes Jungle Jim's puts them on sale for 39 cents a pound.

Beth bakes them in the oven for an hour or so. Then you add a little butter (it doesn't take much, and you can substitute olive oil if you like), brown sugar (again, a couple of teaspoons will be enough) and cinnamon. Delicious. No salt, very little fat (from the butter), and limited sugar.

FERMENTED YOGURT PROTEIN BARS – JANUARY 28, 2018

- Running at the Y with Beth.
- Omelets for dinner.
- I ate one of my fermented Greek yogurt cherry almond vanilla protein bars.
- I originally found them on a trip to Seattle.
- And then I found them again on Amazon.
- I know it sounds disgusting, but they taste great.
- And they have lots of protein.
- And lots of fiber.

The product is Genuine Health Fermented Greek Yogurt Protein+

Bar, Cherry Almond Vanilla. It was the same price on Amazon as the store in Seattle when I posted this. Since then the Amazon price has increased, and the Seattle store has a 10% case discount (which they did all along, I just didn't know about it). But… if we factor in the price of a plane ticket to Seattle, Amazon is the better choice for me.

I'll admit there is a bit of irony that someone who won't touch kale with a ten foot pole likes fermented yogurt, but I do.

JUNGLE JIM'S – FEBRUARY 5, 2018

- Chirp Chips: One cricket per chip. High protein. Taste good only when dipped in hummus. Verdict: Mediocre thing.
- Pork sirloin: Always a great thing on the grill.
- Homemade Ice Cream / Frozen Yogurt (3 for $10). Awesome thing.
- Snickerdoodle hummus. Good thing
- On sale Swiss and Goat cheese. Great things.
- Boar's Head unsalted turkey lunch meat. Great thing
- 3C 2013 Cariñena Red. Go back and get a case great thing.

Boar's Head unsalted turkey lunch meat is the only truly low sodium lunch meat I've ever found. It tastes just like white meat turkey. If you're like me, that means "delicious".

The case of 3C 2013 Cariñena Red came in a wooden box. I split the case with my father in law. Tommy got to keep the box.

The chirp chips wound up being dog treats. Never again.

BICYCLE TRAINERS – FEBRUARY 12, 2017

- I taught Jesse how to fetch.
- Well, labs kind of come with that skill, but I got him to bring the ball back to me 5 times.
- Then when I tried to show his new trick to Beth, Tommy, Kenny and Joe he decided to not do it. Maybe it's not a great thing, but it was hilarious.
- Dinner was… Taco Night!

- Afternoon nap.
- Late in the day I pushed myself to do 30 minutes on the stationary bike.
- It felt great.

To be clear, I don't have a stationary bike. I have a bike, and a bike trainer. I also have a front wheel block to make sure the bike is level. I tried it without the block and it felt like I was biking downhill the whole time. But not in the good coast down the hill kind of way.

I don't have a bike trainer recommendation, since mine is old and no longer sold on Amazon. But Amazon carries several of them for under $100.

MY NEW APPLE WATCH / THE END OF MY FITBIT - FEBRUARY 15, 2018

At the start of the day we had a 15 year old freezer that was starting to fail, and I had a Fitbit with a broken button. So....

- I went to Sam's Club and got an Apple watch.
- Then I went to TV Toastmasters and practiced my contest speech. It's coming together nicely.
- On the way home I stopped at Lee & Jack's TV & Appliances and ordered a new freezer.
- After lunch I swam 30 minutes at the Y.
- The Apple Watch told me how far I swam, and how much of it was freestyle, breaststroke and backstroke.
- I set up the watch with the talking Mickey Mouse watch face.
- Dinner at Beth's parents.
- Paige gave up wine for Lent, so my father in law and I had a glass for her.
- Then we sat in the family room with Tommy and told jokes.

So many great things in one day. Lee and Jacks had the freezer in our garage within two days. The Apple watch tracks steps, albeit more stringently than the Fitbit.

But it also tracks things like run distance, swim distance, active minutes and more.

And any time three generations can sit in the family room and tell jokes, that's the greatest of great things.

A DIET SEMI-TIP – FEBRUARY 20, 2017

- Read more of the two books I'm currently reading: Dream and Grow Rich by Greg Walker, and Getting Things Done by David Allen.
- Kenny, Beth, Tommy and I went to Meijer after dinner.
- Tom picked out some sugar cones.
- I had one with frozen yogurt for a snack.
- It turns out I eat way less frozen yogurt when I put it in a sugar cone.

The average sugar cone has 50 calories in it. And very little sugar. It doesn't hold much ice cream either. The average bowl of ice cream I make for myself has WAY more room for ice cream (or frozen yogurt).

WORKOUT MOTIVATION – APRIL 9, 2018

- Started the day with coffee and a fire in the fireplace.
- Tom and I went to the Y.
- Beth, Tom Joe and I had Chipotle for dinner.
- Got haircuts with Tom at Pete's
- Saw all sorts of cool things at Wrinkles Antiques with Beth and Tom.
- Ended the day with banana milkshakes and a fire in the fireplace

Tommy was on the stationary bike at the Y. He told me he was pretending he was running from zombies - that's how he could go faster and farther.

SHOULDER "THERAPY" – APRIL 10, 2017

- Sunday dinner at Beth's parents' house.
- Low fat blackberry cobbler with ice cream for dessert.
- Took turns telling dumb jokes with my father in law and his neighbor.

- Checked in to my room at the Hilton automatically - one day early, and one floor away from the Fitness Center.

Great thing that happened somewhere between yesterday and today: While wrestling with Joe Barth last night I got my frozen shoulder twisted - and by twisted I mean drop to the ground in screaming pain.

Here's what made that great. Within 5 minutes my shoulder had more mobility than it's had in 3 months. Today I have little to no pain with most of my stretches. Apparently something popped in my shoulder, and it did it in a very good way.

I'm not saying that getting your shoulder twisted in wresting is AMA recommended treatment for frozen shoulder, but it sure worked out for me.

CHIN UPS – MAY 4, 2018

- I counseled the Public Speaking Merit Badge tonight. Some really good speakers with good material!
- Leftover salmon at lunch. With tomatoes and green pepper slices.
- Beth's chili for dinner!
- After breakfast blueberry / strawberry smoothie. I kept my streak of no veggies in the smoothie alive...
- Blackberry wine before bed.
- Did a full chin up.

My lifetime high in chin ups before I turned 55 was (if memory serves) one. Two if I jumped on the second one. I set that record on the ladder in our barn (we can talk safety in another post). That means I set the record when I was roughly 18 years old.

So in late April of 2018 I decided to see if I could at least tie that record. My first attempt was close, I'd say 0.7 of a chin up.

In May I got to one chin up. Eventually I got to two. That set the record.

I still do a couple of chin ups when I work out, but I really haven't felt the need to try for three, or ten, or anything higher. Maybe when I turn 60.

HEALTHY RESTAURANT FOOD – MAY 14, 2016

- LaRosa's spaghetti for dinner.
- I timed the pickup order and got four things at Kroger before getting to La Rosa's, getting the order, and heading back home.
- My father in law delivered the 2015 Raspberry and Blackberry homemade wine (I pick, my mother in law makes it, we split the bottles).
- We talked and had a glass of the 2013 Blackberry while he was here.
- I threw the tennis ball to Riley 4 times. It was a contest to see which one of us would give up first.
    - She won... But she cheated - she ran to the ball, but walked it back to me.

Following my heart attack in 2015, I was put on a diet that (among other things) limited sodium to 1500 mg per day.

To keep things simple I read a label and look for the number of calories to be greater than or equal to the amount of sodium.

I can have (roughly) 2500 calories per day. Some of those calories will be fresh fruit, fresh vegetables or Frosted Mini Wheats (these are sodium free wonders). Making sure I keep the sodium number less than or equal to the calorie number for everything I eat means I will finish under 1500 mg of sodium without really trying.

One area where the sodium tends to be really high is restaurants. In my search to find low sodium and somewhat healthy restaurant food, I've found two go to options: Fish is usually low in sodium and (when grilled) very healthy.

And – at least in the case of LaRosa's and Frisch's Big Boy – spaghetti is a low sodium and not terribly high fat option.

In each of the spaghetti cases I get enough that I eat half for dinner and half later. Also in each case I get a salad to go with it. La Rosa's has an incredible salad. Frisch's has the salad bar so I get what I want.

When it comes to restaurants I always look up the restaurant menu online before I go to dinner. That way I know what I will order before I get there.

In the event the restaurant doesn't have an online menu, I go with fish and ask for no salt. This was also effective when Kenny worked at a restaurant. When he saw the salmon no salt order come back he knew I was there!

WALKING THROUGH THE AIRPORT – JULY 16, 2017

- Good flight to Atlanta.
- Walked for an hour after dinner.
- Late flight to Memphis.

That worked to my advantage, because all the steps from the plane to the rental car to the hotel room were after midnight. - I woke up with 12,000 steps yesterday, and 1200 steps already done for today.

Atlanta's Hartsfield Airport can be a pain to fly through. Or it can be a place to get a nice meal (as mentioned before) and a nice walk.

I try to put 90-120 minutes between my flights in and out of Atlanta. That gives me time to get off the plane (usually in the B or D concourse), go down to the train area and walk one complete loop, all the way out to the F concourse, back to the T concourse, and then to my departure concourse.

Once you get past the D concourse the crowd really thins out. And once you get to the F concourse you can always grab dinner at the Jekyll Island Seafood Company. For something faster there is Fresh to Order in the B concourse.

NOTE: If you aren't a fan of seafood or don't have time for a full meal, Hartsfield has a ton of other options, including Five Guys (a pre heart attack favorite) Chipotle (still a favorite) and Terrapin Brewery (you can't go wrong with a Hopsecutioner).

FROSTED LUCKY CHARMS - SEPTEMBER 20, 2018

- I finished the day with a bowl of Lucky Charms.
- For the first time in four years. - Joe was having a bowl of them, and I said "Wow - looks good"...
- And it was.
- In fact it was magically delicious.
- Best part was I managed to save marshmallows for the last bite.

Given the ratio of calories (110) to sodium (170), Lucky Charms shouldn't be a part of my daily diet. They are more like cigars used to be - maybe one or two a year.

I have cut out cigars completely since the heart attack. That said - I have a Cuban... and when I win the World Championship of Public Speaking... or something equally great happens... I'm going to fire that bad boy up!

OH KALE NO – JANUARY 13, 2018

- Made a quick Kroger run to stock up on the essentials.
- This wasn't a "Oh no bad weather is coming! Get bread and milk!" Kroger run either.
- I didn't buy the kale chips.
- Or the other kale products they had on clearance.

After four years I've learned some things I don't like. At the top of the list is kale.

In the process of researching this book I learned that my great grandparents grew and ate kale. I was told "They were ahead of their time".

Nope. They probably did it to get through the great depression.

My memory of my great grandmother is that she was an incredible cook.

My other memory of her was she made me pancakes, peach pie and served me Neopolitan Ice Cream.

Putting the pieces together I can only come to one conclusion: She knew kale sucked too.

Eventually I did try Kale chips when a Toastmaster friend of mine convinced me to give them a try. When I finally tried Kale chips I learned something about drawing conclusions and hasty judgments.

Sometimes they're correct.

JUNGLE JIM'S – JANUARY 22, 2017

- I woke up a little after 6:00 and played with the puppy.
- I was doing my morning routine at the kitchen table, and he came over.
- I picked him up. He licked my face, yawned three times, and fell asleep while I held him.
- Jungle Jim's after dinner.
- Glass of my in-laws homemade raspberry wine before bed.

Jungle Jim's (www.junglejims.com) is a Cincinnati legend. Need any kind of beer? They probably have it. Wine? Same deal. Ostrich eggs? Really? You need ostrich eggs? How big of a cake are you making? Well, if you do, they have it.

Jungle Jim's started out as a small fruit stand near Hamilton Ohio. Over time it grew to a huge international grocery in Fairfield. When I first moved to the Cincinnati area, I lived a mile from Jungle Jim's. Eventually we moved an hour away from Fairfield.

But then Jungle Jim opened a second store. That store is 15 minutes from our house. It is mentioned frequently in great things.

KASTEEL ROUGE – JANUARY 17, 2018

- Morning nap (i.e. Around 5:45) while holding the puppy (who also

slept).
- Outdoor run in January!
- Beth made pasta for dinner.
- Talked with my father in law after he cut up a bunch of firewood for us. He had a beer (I had to skip because I was getting ready to take Tom to the orthodontist).
- Got a load of split firewood for the cost of one Kasteel Rouge.

I was first introduced to Kasteel Rouge in Memphis by my buddy Jake. It is beer with a nice cherry taste. The next time I was in Jungle Jim's I found a 4 pack of it. Ever since then I've been able to get my fix from Jungle Jim's.

DECAF HIGHLANDER GROGG – APRIL 15, 2018

- A great night's sleep got the day off on the right foot.
- Frosted Mini Wheats for breakfast.
- A 35-minute outdoor run.
- 30 minutes worth of lawn mowing before the sun went down.
- Over 13,000 steps.
- Taco night for dinner!
- Jungle Jim's with Joe which led to...
- $2.99 Amish chicken breast,
- Decaffeinated Highlander Grogg k-cups,
- 4 for $10 12 packs of pop, and
- Blueberry goat cheese, which was how I ended the day.

Jungle Jim's stocks k-cups and regular coffee from LaCrema coffee in West Chester Ohio. That includes my favorite decaf: Highlander Grogg decaf, in k-cup form.

The good news: Even if you don't live near Jungle Jim's you can still get their coffee on Amazon.

The bad news: But (as of this writing), not their k-cups.

TOM AND JUNGLE JIM – FEBRUARY 25, 2017:

- After dinner drip to Jungle Jim's. I found hummus on sale. (Among other things).
- Listened to the book "Getting Things Done" by David Allen. One of my favorites - I like to re-read it every couple of years.

The myth, the legend, the man... and Jungle Jim.

BLACKBERRIES – JULY 25, 2016

- 30 minutes on the stationary bike.
- Taco night for dinner!
- Atari flashback with Tom.
- Watched David Ortiz and the Red Sox
- They lost to the Tigers, and frankly I don't care about that.
- But I love watching the way Ortiz is enjoying his final season. Everyone should enjoy life as much as Big Papi does.
- Got all kinds of things done at work. It was the first day back after two weeks out of the office
- Total amount of blackberries picked just crossed three gallons.

We have blackberries that grow wild all around the edge of our property. I pick them, usually first thing in the morning before it gets hot. Picking has to be done before it gets hot because blackberries have all kinds of thorns. I have to wear jeans and a long sleeve shirt. It's a lot of effort – but worth it.

Because after I pick the blackberries (and freeze them) my in laws come and get them, and turn them into wine.

We split the loot. It has been as many as 10 gallons in a good year.

The same thing happens with the black raspberries that grow on our property in June, with a couple of exceptions: We've never done much more than a gallon, and they don't grow wild. The vines were planted around 70 years ago and continue to bloom every year.

BILLY JOEL AND KALE – JUNE 1, 2017

- Let's start here: I've been beating up on kale recently
- With good reason - it tastes terrible.
- But... Today I had a spinach and kale salad with Farmer's Market goat cheese, and the goat cheese covered up the taste of kale. Huge win. (If you love goat cheese).
- 30 minutes on the bike...with Billy Joel.
- Which is to say I listened to Billy Joel while riding the stationary bike.
- Mind you I would definitely go bike riding with Billy Joel. Even a tandem.
- And I'd let him steer if he wanted.

When I gathered the material for the book I was shocked to find out that there was one time when I didn't out and out hate kale.

That said, I still believe that kale tastes like dirt. And you either cover it up (with goat cheese) or you eat dirt.

If I'm going to cover up something with goat cheese I'd rather it was spinach. Or spaghetti. Or a dog treat.

Basically anything other than kale.

LET'S EAT! AND EXERCISE

THE GREAT COFFEE DRAFT – NOVEMBER 22, 2018

- Grilled swordfish and burgers for dinner.
- With baked sweet potatoes!
- Beth and I had lunch together - scrambled eggs and toast.
- Tom, Beth and I conducted the great K Cup coffee draft.

We got a 12 pack of K Cups at Jungle Jim's. The next day we had our K Cup draft.

We picked in order of age, so I had the number one pick. There really was no Myles Garrett / Baker Mayfield type pick, so I offered Tom a trade down.

He didn't see a franchise K Cup either, so he declined.

Draft results are on the packaging. What's not shown are the three we already drank: Butter rum (Tom), Santa's Blend (Beth) and Roasted Chestnut (Phil).

The K Cups were so good we bought two more packs. One for us and one for a gift.

LET'S EAT! AND EXERCISE

10 | THE RECIPES

After four years of watching my diet and three years of collecting all great things Beth and I have come up with some great recipes. Mostly Beth.

Here are the favorites:

BUDDY BOYS – FEBRUARY 1, 2017:

- Beth made buddy boys for dinner.
- Read more of the book "Change Your Brain, Change Your Life".
- Just saw Auto-correct try to change the title to Change Your Brain Change Your Lice.
- Anyway, the book said that a brain activity study showed that listening to Mozart improves creativity.
- Listened to Mozart.
- (It might take multiple days to have the full effect).

Beth's Buddy Boy recipe:

Buns, ham lunch meat (we use low sodium), Swiss cheese (which is also low in sodium).

Put the ham and Swiss on the buns and place them in the oven long enough to melt the cheese.

Bring them out, add tomato slices and olive oil mayo.

BANANA BREAD RECIPE - FEBRUARY 13, 2017

- Got some speech feedback from Michael Davis - great stuff!
- Beth made meatloaf for dinner - also great stuff!
- All five of us watched the first episode of 24 Legacy (we had it recorded).
- Beth made banana bread for our during the show snack.
- I dropped off five boxes of clothing, books, etc. at the Goodwill Donation center.
- Had a great conversation with the attendant, who grew up in Cleveland.
- Walked outside.

Beth's Banana Bread Recipe (makes one loaf)

Ingredients:
½ cup melted butter
½ cup sugar
2 eggs
1 cup mashed ripe banana
2 cups flour
½ tsp salt
1 tsp baking soda
1/3 cup hot water

Directions:
In a large bowl combine butter and sugar. Then mix in eggs and banana, blending until smooth.
Add flour, salt and baking soda until thoroughly blended.

Add hot water.
Spoon batter into a greased 9 by 5 inch pan.
Bake in preheated 325 degree oven for 1 hour 10 minutes or until bread begins to pull away from sides of pan.
Let cool in pan for 10 minutes.
Turn out on to a rack to cool completely.

BANANA MILKSHAKES – FEBRUARY 27, 2018

- I read a list of ideas: Things to give up for Lent.
- One of them was procrastination.
- Tommy said "I'm going to give that up next year".
- Big progress on a work initiative.
- Banana milkshakes with Beth before bed.

Banana milkshakes are mentioned frequently in Great Things. Here is the recipe:

Ingredients:
One ripe banana, the riper the better. (To a certain extent...)
(Note: Frozen ripe bananas work well too).
2-3 scoops of vanilla frozen yogurt. Kroger is a personal favorite, but any kind will work.
6 ounces (more or less) of 1% milk.
Put it in the blender and mix it up.

You can also add cinnamon if you like (and I do).

Additional note on frozen bananas: To freeze them you need to cut them up, and freeze the individual slices for about 90 minutes (A little more if they're really ripe). I put them on a tray lined with parchment paper. After 90 minutes put them in a freezer bag. This keeps them from sticking together when they freeze.

The same advice applies for freezing pineapple.

GREAT BURGERS – MARCH 6, 2017

- Kenny and I had an after dinner glass of wine and talked about music.
- Ran on the treadmill.
- Grilled Laura's Lean burgers for dinner.
- Got our taxes finished.

If you don't have access to Jungle Jim's (specifically their Star Ranch Angus meat counter) Laura's Lean beef ground beef is as good as it gets. And if you grab it at Sam's Club, you can get it at a good price (as long as you're willing to buy in large quantities).

If you do have access to Jungle Jim's, then the 85/15 ground sirloin form the Star Ranch Angus meat counter is amazing.

In any case… here's my burger recipe

Take half of your burger patty and put it in the burger press (and press it).
Add Worcestershire sauce and garlic.
Add the other half of the burger patty and press it together.

(One additional great thing: Spell check knows how to spell the word Worcestershire. Now if only it could help me pronounce the word…)

DIRT DESSERT – MARCH 24, 2018

- Dinner with my in laws.
- Beth made pasta bake, veggies and dirt dessert.
- Paige made bread.
- I opened wine.
- The weather was pretty much perfect. I got to run outdoors.

Beth's awesome Dirt Dessert Recipe

Ingredients:
8 ounce package cream cheese (low fat works, fat free does not)
16 ounces of Oreo cookies
16 ounces low fat Cool Whip (fat free not as good)
2 packages instant vanilla pudding
3 cups 2% milk

Directions:
Mix cream cheese and cool whip together.
Add pudding, milk and blend.
Crush Oreos. Mix in some, add the rest on top.
Chill in the fridge for at least two hours (overnight is even better).

OMELETS AND MORE – MARCH 26, 2017

- Took 2 walks with the puppy.
- Second one was with puppy, Kenny and Beth.
- Over 10,000 steps.
- Omelets for dinner.
- Watched some good NCAA basketball games.
- Read more of the book Superforecasting.
- Beth made incredible banana bread for a snack.

I make two kinds of omelets: The fluffy one for family, and the near egg white kind for me.

Recipe for the fluffy (3-2-1) omelet:
Three brown eggs (white ones also work, but we get really nice brown eggs from a neighbor).
Two tablespoons milk.
One tablespoon Bisquik.

THE RECIPES

Recipe for the mostly egg white omelet:
Four brown eggs.
Two egg whites only (separate out the yolk for later use).
Two full eggs.
I add spinach, goat cheese, garlic, mushrooms and tarragon to my omelet.

BLUEBERRY MILKSHAKES - APRIL 16, 2016

- Judged a scholarship competition with Beth Barth and Cassie Anderson.
- Got a nice pin and stitched flag as unexpected but really nice thank you gifts.
- Mowed more of the lawn. Over 14,000 steps for the day.
- Got another ton of gravel down - in under one hour - thanks to Kenny, Joe and Tom for all their help. (Literally, it was one ton of gravel).
- Burned up a bunch of branches and limbs
- Watched Star Wars VII with Beth, Joe and Tom.
- Made all kinds of Star Trek references during the movie like "Is Jean Luc Picard in this one?"
- Unsalted air popped popcorn with the movie.
- And milkshakes: Banana for Beth, Blueberry for me.

Blueberry Milkshake Recipe

Ingredients:
- Frozen blueberries – a generous amount (I get about ¾ cup.)
- 2-3 scoops of vanilla frozen yogurt.
- 6 ounces (more or less) of 1% milk.
- 1 teaspoon of Stonewall Kitchen Maine Wild Blueberry Jam (this is the key).

Directions:

Put it in the blender and mix it up. Stonewall Kitchen Maine Wild Blueberry Jam is available at LL Bean, or (of course) Jungle Jim's.

GRILLED SALMON– MAY 2, 2016

- Ran 30 minutes.
- Listened to Zig Ziglar while I ran.
- Got some hummus at Meijer. (I was out).
- Found some spots in the yard that were dry enough to mow.
- Showed Tommy how to build his own play list on the iPad.
- Grilled salmon for dinner.
- Watched Tom as he rode a 3D VR roller coaster using my iPhone and Google glasses.

If I were to do a word cloud on this book, I would imagine salmon would be a big one. That and banana milkshakes. (I'd have to restrict it to nouns only, because I don't want "The" or "Ran" to show up.) (And nouns – not pronouns or proper names).

But I digress.

Here is my salmon recipe:

Ingredients:
1/3 cup Jim Beam bourbon
1/3 cup Low sodium soy sauce
1/2 cup brown sugar
2 tbsp Oil

If it's direct on the grill I do 8 minutes for the grilling (for a 1 inch thick piece), skin side down.

If I'm grilling it on a cedar plank (which is soaked in water for 30 minutes prior to grilling), I go for 10 minutes.

I normally go with wild salmon. I'm not fanatical about it. I keep some frozen salmon around – and that is sometimes farm raised. I know it's not as good as wild caught, but it's still better than hot dogs. (A high standard I know)

VANILLA MILKSHAKES - MAY 5, 2017

- Saw Beth's cousin Chris at Meijer - he had his daughter tell me I was wearing the wrong sweatshirt.
- Did I mention that the weather was cool enough to wear my chief Wahoo sweatshirt?
- Speaking of which - It didn't involve me, but it's still great that the Indians swept the Tigers for a second time in a row. I can't remember the last time they went 6-0 against Detroit.
- Found two really ripe bananas at Meijer, which were perfect in our two evening milkshakes.
- Tom skipped banana and had vanilla.

Vanilla Milkshake Recipe

Ingredients:
A little bit of vanilla. Imitation vanilla is fine.
1 teaspoon of sugar
2-3 scoops of vanilla frozen yogurt.
6 ounces (more or less) of 1% milk.

Put it in the blender and mix it up.

TACO PIE - MAY 10, 2016

- 30 minute presentation to my boss's boss only took 15 minutes.
- And at the end he said "Great stuff".
- Attended Tommy's middle school awards banquet.
- Frisch's afterwards to celebrate.
- Found out that Frisch's makes good smoothies.
- 30 minutes on the bike.
- Beth made taco pie for dinner.

- All five of us were here for dinner.
- And the taco pie got five thumbs up!

Beth's Impossibly Easy Taco Pie Recipe:

Ingredients:
1 pound ground turkey or beef
1 envelope taco seasoning mix
½ cup Bisquick
1 cup milk
2 eggs
½ cup shredded cheddar cheese
Salsa, if desired
Sour cream, if desired

Directions:
Preheat oven to 400 degrees. Grease or spray 9 inch pie pan.
Brown ground meat, drain fat, and stir in taco seasoning mix. Spread in bottom of pie pan.
Stir Bisquick, milk, and eggs until blended. Pour into pie plate.
Bake for 25 minutes.
Top with cheese and bake 3 more minutes.
Remove from oven and let stand 5 minutes before serving.
Serve with salsa and sour cream.

FARMER'S BREAKFAST – MAY 17, 2017

- 30 minutes on the elliptical.
- Kenny and Tom made dinner.
- It was Farmer's Breakfast, and it was delicious.
- Watched some of the Cavaliers imitation of the Harlem Globetrotters (and the Toronto Raptors imitation of the Washington Generals).

Farmer's Breakfast Recipe:

Ingredients:
One pound Sausage (we normally use turkey sausage),
Ore Ida Potatoes O'Brien (one bag)
2-3 eggs per person (we use a dozen for five).

Directions:
Brown the sausage in a pan.
Add the Potatoes O'Brien and cook them until they are light brown.
Add the eggs and cook them until they're done.

Serve with tortillas and cheese or maple syrup. Or 0both.

Farmer's Breakfast works as a camping meal, or a dinner. Or breakfast. We add milk with the eggs at home. That doesn't always happen on campouts. When we cook the sausage at home we drain the fat. That also doesn't always happen on campouts.

TWO FOR ONE - MAY 20, 2017

- Grilled boneless pork chops, metts and brats.
- Kenny brought some cheesy jalapeno metts to the party as well - they were a huge hit.
- Beth made her crock pot macaroni and cheese and chocolate chews. Both were incredible!
- Tommy helped me with the grilling.
- We got the food done just before the thunderstorm broke loose.
- It was also an early birthday party for Joe. The official (19th) birthday party is coming!

Creamy Crock Pot Mac and Cheese Recipe:

Ingredients:
2 cups uncooked elbow macaroni or medium shells
4 tablespoons (1/2 stick) butter, cut into pieces
1 cup grated Cheddar cheese

1/2 cup sour cream
1 (10 3/4-ounce) can condensed Cheddar cheese soup
1 cup milk

Directions:
Boil the pasta until tender, about 8 minutes. Drain.
In a medium saucepan, melt butter on low heat and stir in cheese until it melts. Add in sour cream and soup.
In a crock pot, combine cheese sauce and drained macaroni. Add milk and stir well.
Set the crock pot on low setting and cook for 3 hours, stirring occasionally.

Note: Double this recipe to fill a large crock pot.

Chocolate Chews Recipe:

Ingredients:
1 ¼ cups flour
1 teaspoon baking powder
½ teaspoon cinnamon
¼ teaspoon salt
½ cup softened butter
1 ¼ cups firmly packed brown sugar
1 teaspoon vanilla extract
2 eggs
1 cup chocolate chips

Directions:
Preheat oven to 350 degrees.
In small bowl, combine flour, baking powder, cinnamon, and salt; set aside.
In large bowl combine butter, brown sugar, and vanilla extract. Beat until creamy.
Add eggs one at a time, beating well after each addition.
Gradually blend in flour mixture, then chocolate chips.

Spread evenly in greased 13 x 9 inch baking pan. Bake 18 minutes.

JOE'S BIRTHDAY / BETH'S PUMPKIN PIE – MAY 23, 2017

- Beth's pumpkin pie for dessert!

When you have pie instead of cake for a birthday - that's some good pie.

It's been mentioned several times. **Here is my wife's pumpkin pie recipe:**

Ingredients:
2 15 ounce cans of pumpkin.
1 1/2 cups firmly packed light brown sugar.
4 eggs, well beaten.
3 tbsp butter (melted).
2 tbsp dark cooking syrup.
1 tbsp pumpkin pie spice.
1 1/4 tsp salt.
1 1/4 cups milk or diluted evaporated milk.
Unbaked pastry pie crusts.

Directions:
Combine pumpkin, sugar and remaining ingredients in the order given.
Bake in a pre-heated 450 degree oven for 10 minutes.
Reduce heat in oven to 325 (leave door slightly ajar for three minutes) and continue baking for 45 minutes to 1 hour.

If you don't have pumpkin pie spice use 2 tsp of cinnamon, 3/4 tsp of ginger and 1/2 tsp nutmeg.

MEATLOAF - JULY 3, 2018

- Ran on the track at the Y.

- Beth made meatloaf, carrots, broccoli and mac and cheese for dinner.
- Plus apple pie and vanilla frozen yogurt for dessert.
- Organized the wine cellar.
- Determined that having wine racks in the basement qualifies as a "wine cellar".
- Started the reorganization of my grill area.
- Got the new license plates on Joe's car.
- Blueberry light ice cream with extra blueberries for a bedtime snack.
- Watched an episode of The Librarians with Tom and Beth.

Beth's Meatloaf Recipe:

Ingredients:
1 pound ground turkey or beef
One 8 oz. can tomato sauce
1 cup oats
1 egg
2 pounds raw carrots

Directions
Mix ground meat, tomato sauce, oats, and egg.
Scrape mixture into the center of a roaster or Dutch oven and form into a loaf with a spatula.
Peel, then cut carrots into 2 to 3 inch pieces and place all around the loaf.
Cover the bottom of the pan with water.
Cover the pan with a lid and bake for 1 hour at 350 degrees.

GRILLED PEACHES AND ICE CREAM – JULY 24, 2016

- Smoothie with a fresh peach, banana, protein powder and orange juice.
- Walk with Beth, Kenny, Joe and Tom at the end of the day to get to 10,000 steps.
- Afternoon at the pool with Beth and Tom.
- Grilled pork chops for dinner.

- With grilled peaches and ice cream for dessert. (As featured on the Vlog).
- Family movie night: Terminator Genisys.

Grilled peach dessert recipe:

Ingredients:
Peaches (one for every two servings)
Olive oil spray
Brown Sugar
Cinnamon
Vanilla frozen yogurt (or ice cream)

Cut peaches in half, spray with olive oil.
Put brown sugar and cinnamon on the peaches.
Put the peaches cut side down on the grill for 5 minutes. (Around 350 degrees)
Move them to indirect heat for another 5 minutes.
Take them off the grill, put them in a bowl and add ice cream.

RIB RUB RECIPE – AUGUST 15, 2016

- Made it to Suffolk safely.
- Had a great dinner at the hotel.
- Got some good rib grilling tips from Carmen.
- Got to bed early, which is great because tomorrow is an early one…

I won't share the tips from my co-worker Carmen, since she and her husband Todd enter the Memphis barbeque festival ribs contest every year. They compete against people who are barbeque professionals (I didn't know there was such a thing). And they do quite well.

But I can share my rib rub recipe:

Ingredients
1 cup Brown Sugar, packed.

1 ½ tsp cinnamon
½ tsp or so of nutmeg.
(The prior 2 are a substitute for allspice. I use allspice if I have it).
1 tsp cayenne pepper (optional).
2 tbsp garlic,
1 tbsp freshly ground black pepper.
1 ½ tsp Cumin.
1 ½ tsp coffee.

I smoke my ribs on the gas grill with mesquite chips, and – even though I've read it doesn't make a lot of difference – I use the Texas crutch (put the ribs in foil with a mixture of half apple juice and half water) for 30 minutes.

I realize what I just said is – to rib professionals – sacrilege.

But these ribs are great, because of what I do in the end…

VERMONT PIG CANDY - SEPTEMBER 5, 2017

- Labor Day holiday!
- Got some of the lawn mowed.
- Got rid of the limb that fell off in the last storm. Fire pit.
- Made ribs for dinner.
- Picked some tomatoes from my in law's garden.
- Planned out my day tomorrow.

The biggest benefit of using the Texas Crutch is this: It gives me the raw material to make Vermont Pig Candy.

There are a variety of ways to do this, but it boils down (pun intended) to this:

After doing the Texas Crutch, take the liquid from the foil and put it in a sauce pan (at this point it's apple juice, water and pork drippings).
Boil it until you have roughly 1/3 of the original liquid. This tends to be about 1/3 cup.

Add 1/4 cup of dark brown real maple syrup and boil until it foams. (You can then add salt and/or hot sauce if you like. I leave it as is.) Coat the ribs with the mixture.

LONDON BROIL – OCTOBER 9, 2016

- Ran on the treadmill.
- Got 12,000 steps.
- 8 track flashback: Steve Martin: "Comedy is Not Pretty". Not as funny as "A Wild and Crazy Guy", but still very funny.
- Beth and I hit Kroger after dinner.
- They had huge boxes of Frosted Mini Wheats on sale.
- I got a really nice London Broil on sale. It goes on the grill tomorrow!

Phil's London Broil Recipe: This works with a cut labeled London Broil, or a Sirloin. In fact, I prefer sirloin, because it's not quite as thick.

Ingredients:
Steak
Garlic
Pepper
Worcestershire sacue

Directions:
Pull the steak out of the refrigerator and bring it to room temperature before you broil. This loosens up the muscles, tendons, etc. in the meat. You don't run cold, so don't grill steak cold either.
Rub the steak with garlic, pepper and Worcestershire sauce.
Grill at 400. 7-9 minutes. (Depending on the thickness and how done you like your steak.)
Take it off for 10 minutes after grilling.
Slice the steak at a 45 degree angle, against the grain.

SHRIMP SKEWERS – OCTOBER 13, 2017

- Grilled shrimp skewers for dinner.

This is one of our favorite grill recipes, and one of the easiest. I get fresh shrimp when possible, but frozen also works (just thaw it first).

Ingredients:
Shrimp
Turkey kielbasa
Fresh mushrooms
Green peppers
Pineapple

Since the kielbasa is pre-cooked the only thing to watch is the shrimp. When they turn pink you're done. It doesn't take long.

If you're getting fresh shrimp you will also need a de-veiner.
If on a low sodium diet check the label on any frozen shrimp. Sodium varies wildly.

We have also done cherry tomatoes, but they tend to cook faster than the other items. We fix that by giving them their own skewers.

Small potatoes and onions are also favorites. Our strategy with both is to cook them in olive oil. Both take longer than the rest of the skewers to fully cook.

BANANAS FOSTER AND MORE – NOVEMBER 27, 2016

- Another nerf dart war with Joe.
- Got more Christmas shopping done online.
- Fourth of four Thanksgiving weekend family dinners: Grilled pork chops, baked sweet potatoes, vegetables, fruit salad.
- And for dessert - grilled bananas foster.
- The bananas foster was an experiment. It was a successful experiment - and it has been added to the rotation.

Bananas Foster Recipe

Ingredients:
1/3 cup black rum (NOT 151 proof)
1/4 cup brown sugar.
1/2 tsp pumpkin pie spice
1/2 tsp cinnamon.
Bananas.

Directions:
Stir up the rum, brown sugar, pumpkin pie spice and cinnamon.
Cut up bananas and marinate the pieces in the mix (I only did this for a minute or so - I didn't want to wait).

Grill the bananas for about 6 minutes. I put them on a copper grate. (Next time I will go non-stick on the grate).

After pulling the bananas off the grill, pour the rest of the rum mix over them. (Use a fire safe plate) And light it. Carefully.

This is why you don't use 151. Regular rum will light just fine and make a nice blue flame. 151 could burn your house down.

OKAY, I ATE A DOG TREAT - DECEMBER 20, 2018

- First day of Christmas vacation!
- Tommy and I worked out at the Y.
- Grilled chicken and tilapia (two separate courses, not together) plus baked sweet potatoes for dinner.
- Paige made dog treats out of pumpkin and more.
- And Tom and I broke our resolution about never eating dog treats.
- Verdict: Good stuff.

Paige's Dog Treat Recipe

Ingredients:
¾ cup canned pumpkin
2 ½ cups flour
½ teaspoon salt
2 tablespoons dried milk powder
¼ cup water
2 eggs

Directions:
Preheat oven to 350 degrees.
Mix all ingredients together.
Spray cookie sheet with cooking spray.
Roll out dough to ½" thick and cut with small cookie cutters; then place on cookie sheet. Or, press into cookie sheets with molds.
Bake 20 minutes, then flip and bake another 20 minutes on other side.

Makes about 20 biscuits, depending on size of cutters/molds. They are larger than a normal dog biscuit.

CHICKEN SALAD RECIPE – DECEMBER 21, 2017:

- Beth turned our leftover grilled chicken and grapes into chicken salad for our lunch.
- We went to the Y.
- I introduced Tommy to the album "Wish You Were Here" while we were riding to Eastgate.

Beth's Chicken Salad Recipe:

Ingredients:
1 pound deli rotisserie chicken
1 cup green or red seedless grapes
3 - 4 tablespoons olive oil mayonnaise
Black pepper corns
Dried orange peel

Directions:
Cut chicken into bite sized pieces and add to bowl.
Cut grapes in half and add to chicken.
Add mayo – more or less depending on how you like it.
Add ½ teaspoon dried orange peel.
Grind black pepper and season to taste.
Gently mix all ingredients.
Chill for 30 minutes.

NOTE: Leftover grilled chicken can be cut up if you don't have deli rotisserie chicken, but it's not as good. It's still pretty good though.

11 | HUMOR

From funny TV shows and movies to the recently popular "Dad jokes", humor is one of the best stress busters ever. (We could argue about whether dad jokes qualify as humor, but it's my book and I'm a dad).

What follows is some of the Great Things Humor moments plus a section of my favorite dad jokes (feel free to skip that if you like).

SNOW DAYS AND PHANTOM FARTS – JANUARY 5, 2017

- Snow day - worked from home.
- Made it over to the Y with Tommy.
- Tom and I also did our first Great Things Facebook Live.
- And no - I didn't. (if you saw the video). I brought this one on myself.

I convinced Tom to do a Facebook Live for our vlog. Before we got started he said "What if we mess something up?" I said "How bad can it be? We might have a couple of people watching. We can always delete the video after."

All he heard was "How bad can it be?" He said "Well, what if I fart?" I said "Just blame it on me."

The whole time we were talking the wheels in his head were turning.

Sure enough, not too long before we finished, Tom asked the question: "Dad, did you fart?"

No I didn't. As far as I know, no one did.

TECH TIP - FEBRUARY 19, 2018:

- Ran on the track at the Y with Beth.
- After dinner walk with Beth and Tommy.
- No problem getting 10,000 steps.

Here's a tech tip that can keep you out of potential trouble. When you are in camera mode on your phone, and listening to music, the lower volume photo will snap a picture. And hitting the button repeatedly will NOT turn down the volume, it will just keep snapping pictures.

So let's just say... for the sake of argument, you had snapped a picture of geese in the YMCA pool... and then you walked in to the locker room and decided to turn down your music...

Well, you'd be really glad that you already knew that tip.

Or that your phone was pointed at the floor.

ACTING UP IN STORES – FEBRUARY 17, 2016

- Treadmill and weights at the fitness center.
- But not at the same time.
- Dinner at Chipotle.
- Tommy didn't feel well (getting a cold) so we brought him home a burrito.
- Kenny had to work, so we brought him home a burrito.
- It was kind of like Oprah. "You get a burrito! And you get a burrito!"
- After dinner we went to GFS and got things for Blue and Gold banquet.
- And Joe and I acted up.

The exact details of how we acted up in GFS are irrelevant. Suffice it to say they were not illegal, involved as many puns as we could generate, and perhaps putting things in the cart that Beth was not expecting.

Acting up. It's what Joe and I do. It all goes back to that time in Odd Lots when Joe was about 6 years old, and we played catch with a nerf-like football in the middle of the aisle. ("Nerf-like" as opposed to Nerf... it was Odd Lots).

In the end we bought the football at Odd Lots. It just seemed like the right thing to do. For one thing, we could always take it to Odd Lots the next time - because they might be out.

SAFETY DANCE – MARCH 8, 2017

- I gave a safety presentation.
- That meant I got to reference some 80s music, like:
- Safety Dance (opening slide).
- And Keep Your Hands to Yourself (closing slide).
- And Love in an Elevator, which was actually the 90s, but still - it's Aerosmith...
- And as I noted in the presentation, my closing slide also works if I need to give a Sexual Harassment seminar.

A word of explanation: Both Love in an Elevator, and Keep Your Hands to Yourself were related to the safety observation that people tend to put their hands in between closing elevator doors instead of using the door open button - a low injury likelihood, but very large injury if something goes wrong.

THE DARK SIDE OF LENT – MARCH 19, 2017

- Beth made crock pot mac and cheese and baked sweet potatoes.
- I grilled salmon and burger patties.
- Note: That prior entry is two separate things. A patty made of salmon and burger would be disgusting.

- Additional note: The salmon was just salmon. Not a patty at all. Salmon patties are also disgusting.
- Well it was salmon with brown sugar, Jim Beam, low sodium soy sauce and a little oil. But you get the idea.

Okay, where was I? Oh yeah

- Everyone was here for the feast.
- It was Sunday, so I washed it down with Diet Mt. Dew.

I gave up soft drinks for Lent in 2017. That wasn't easy, but it wasn't the most difficult thing I've ever given up. I gave up ice cream for Lent one year (including frozen yogurt). That also wasn't easy, but it wasn't the most difficult thing I've ever given up.

I gave up sarcasm for Lent one year.

Never again.

STRAIGHT OUT OF AIRPLANE! - MARCH 23, 2018

- Beth, Tommy and I watched a show about a guy who was looking for German gold in a deep lake in Namibia.
- I learned they have a really neat Oktoberfest in Namibia.
- I also learned that he found a German cannon, but...
- I didn't learn about the gold - because I fell asleep.
- Finished the Book "Do Over" by Jon Acuff. Great advice and hilarious. Highly recommend it.
- Grilled chicken with a new no-salt rub for dinner.

Kudos to Tommy for the following exchange:

Beth: Did you get money for the volleyball game?
Phil (Surprised that they have a volleyball game out of season): What's the volleyball game?

Tommy: Well they put this net in the middle of the gym, and two teams get on either side...

GOOD OMELETS – APRIL 12, 2016

- Ran on the treadmill before breakfast.
- Had a good omelet (that hadn't hit the floor - I think).
- Breakfast was comped. Even though I'm on a business trip and it would have been paid for anyway - there's just something about getting free food...
- Great lunch catered in at the mill. Tilapia and broccoli salad.
- And a small brownie.
- Found a local place that had salmon for dinner. Lots of fish getting eaten this week.
- Really productive meetings. Nothing like a project deadline to make people focus and move the meetings along.
- Met a lot of really nice people at the Riegelwood mill.

I asked the server why my omelet was taking so long. She said "Oh he dropped it on the floor." I hope she meant "he dropped the first one on the floor…"

FUTURE ZOMBIE HEADS – APRIL 26, 2018

- I didn't have enough Frosted Mini Wheats for a full bowl, so I had a strawberry / banana / blueberry / etc. smoothie to go with them.
- Got some shoulder lifts, regular lifts and elliptical work done.
- Gave a speech at Toastmasters - and got outstanding feedback from Michael J Pope Jr.
- Also got to hear a great speech by the same Mr. Pope - and had a really good chat with him and Randy after the meeting.
- Beth and I did some shopping for the upcoming zombie themed campout. Including getting "zombie heads".

- And that got us some very interesting looks at Michael's

COURT OF HONOR HUMOR - APRIL 27, 2016

- Got the missing health credits issue resolved.
- Had a great court of honor with a lot of laughs.
- Realized that - even when I mess up and give the wrong award to a scout - everyone has a great sense of humor about it.
- Got a great laugh at the court of honor when my son Joe called me Steve Harvey.
- Good conversation with parents after the COH.
- 30 minutes on the bike.
- Got everything done in time to get to bed early... Right after a glass of blackberry wine.

Three to four times a year a Boy Scout troop holds the Court of Honor. This formal event recognizes progress made by the scouts. The formality of the event can be somewhat compromised when the

Scoutmaster (that would be me) recognizes the wrong scout for an award.

Fortunately (I guess) my son Joe immediately broke the ice by calling me Steve Harvey. This was not long after Steve Harvey temporarily crowned Miss Columbia the winner of the Miss Universe pageant when it was actually Miss Philippines.

PARROTS – APRIL 30, 2016

GREAT QUOTE I READ: "Your language should be so clean you could give your talkative parrot to a priest, preacher or rabbi." (From Zig Ziglar, but he was quoting someone else).

GREAT THINGS THAT HAPPENED

- Got the mulch down at Harmony Hill - Finished just before the rain started.
- Tommy made cheesecake cupcakes for desert, fulfilling another cooking merit badge requirements.
- I got 30 minutes in on the elliptical.
- I had my first "Zig-a-thon". I flipped the day's script and played music on the drive, and Zig Ziglar at the office.
- I traded the highway for back roads on the drive to work. Much more fun.
- I still made it to work in the same amount of time.

SOMETHING I AM GRATEFUL FOR - I don't have a talkative parrot.

THAT 70S SHOW – MAY 8, 2017

- Mother's Day dinner at Paige's with friends and family.

- Lasagna for the dinner (whole wheat pasta) + salad, brussels sprouts, and homemade apple pie for dessert.
- Made a silk purse (a new storage idea for the house) out of a sow's ear (cleaning up some water in the basement).
- Great phone conversation with my mom.
- I threw the tennis ball up against the garage 8 times. Overhand.
- Watched That 70s Show with Beth, Joe and Tom...
- And had banana milkshakes.

One of the things I like about shows in syndication. It gives me a chance to watch shows I might have missed the first time around. Case in point "That 70s Show". The first time I ever saw the show was 2001, (that would have been season four) when Beth was in labor for Tom.

Wow, that sounded terrible. Let me explain. They were inducing labor on December 26. We had a large room with a TV, so I turned it on and... Nope, still sounds terrible. Moving on.

I have no idea why we didn't watch it the first time around, but we didn't. We did, however, start watching it in rerun. And it's hilarious.

The fact that it's still in syndication when our sons are 17, 21 and 24 means they can enjoy the humor as well.

A JOKE AT CHIPOTLE – MAY 22, 2018

- We ran in to our friends Jason and Angela and family at Chipotle. They were on their way to the Reds Indians game.
- Angela gave us two buy one get one free coupons!
- Jason helped me pull a prank on Tommy Barth.

The prank: In the middle of our dinner Tommy burped. I said "Wow was that loud!". Jason was seated across the restaurant. I texted him "Hey when Tom comes over to say hi ask him if he burped."

Tom went over to say hi, then came back and said "Jason heard my burp!" "Told you it was loud." Tom didn't realize it was a joke until he saw it on Great Things.

REMEMBERING TOYS R US – JUNE 25, 2016

- Got Joe's new (for him) Civic.
- It was 90+ degrees, so Beth and I hit the pool.
- Beth, Tom and I went to Panera for dinner.
- We used a gift card, so it was free.
- We also went to Kohl's, where we spent EXACTLY our Kohl's cash.
- We stopped at Toys R Us
- Tom found some cool Schleich figures on sale - and again... he had a gift card.
- I almost got busted creating one of my famous "animal death scenes" with the Schleich figures...
- We finished our shopping day at Ollie's, where I found K-Cups and fluorescent bulbs for a fraction of what they normally cost.

I can't say I miss Toys R Us. But I do miss moments like this:

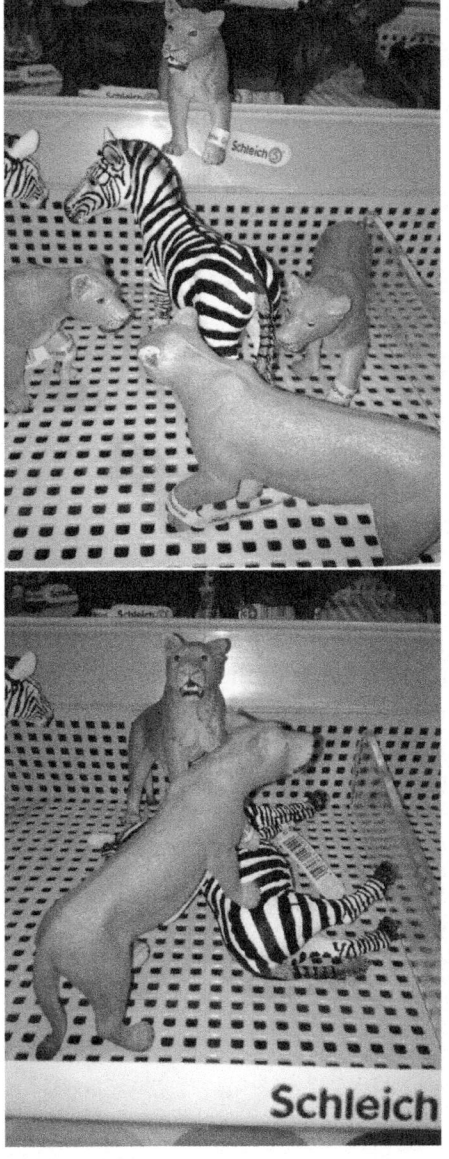

PULP FICTION - JUNE 26, 2016

- Bailey and I started a new morning routine. She waits on the rug, until I sit on the floor to read. Then she sits down next to me, and eventually lays down.
- Also got her to bark like crazy when I asked her if she wanted to play ball.
- Listened to The Kinks with Tom on the way to Eastgate.
- The look on Tom's face as the light when on and he said

"WAIT A MINUTE... IS LOLA... A..."

- The Indians swept their third consecutive series. They haven't lost since the Cavs won the NBA championship.
- The Cavs are still the NBA champions.
- Got in an indoor run at the Y.

The perfect example of a small great moment: I put my k-cup in the brewer at work. I pressed the button. I then went to the restroom. When I got back to the brewer, it was just finishing up my cup.

After I posted it on Facebook there was a string of "Pulp Fiction" replies back and forth.

Beth said "Don't you just love it when you come back from the bathroom and find your food waiting for you?"

My friend Russ said "You need to get her a Five Dollar Milk Shake for that."

MONTY PYTHON – JUNE 27, 2016

- Helped kids walk on water... Well corn starch helped too... (with my friend Joe).
- While we were talking with the kids at Vacation Bible School, we had the following exchange:

JOE: Everyone is scared of something. Phil, what are you scared of?
PHIL: The Spanish Inquisition.
JOE: Nobody expected that.
Then we paused and looked out the door...

- Enjoyed a moment of complete silence after that joke.
- Remembered that women and children don't always enjoy Monty Python jokes.

MACK DADDY AND MORE – JUNE 29, 2016

- The Indians won 12 in a row - first time in my lifetime they've done that.
- The troop organized the trailer.
- Then we made s'mores.
- Spinach salad and salmon for lunch.
- Tom said "Have you ever felt like someone was watching you?" This allowed me to break into an 80s song... Always great fun for me. "I always feel like... somebody's watching me..." (Rockwell) #dadjokes
- We found a baby raccoon in our garage. He was cute.
- We relocated him back to the wild (and gave him some dog food for dinner).
- Beth called the Health Department to ask what to do if a raccoon was rabid (this one wasn't). The response gave us both a really good laugh.
- The response: Cut off the raccoon's head and we will check it. Uh... no.

- Looked up "Mack Daddy" on Urban Dictionary - because Tom asked me what it meant when they said it on a rerun of Big Bang Theory, and I didn't know... But now I do.

Mack Daddy: A man of superior looks. A player of players. A romantic lady killer.

TOM'S NEW PACMAN SUIT – AUGUST 12, 2018

- Beth and I ran at the Y.
- Tommy and I assembled two bench seats for his Eagle Scout project.
- Then the 3 of us had dinner at Bob Evans. Beth ordered the flounder, I ordered the salmon.
- They brought us two flounders. When I mentioned it the waiter apologized and said keep the flounder I'll have them make you a salmon.
- So I got a fresh hot piece of salmon, and Beth has a piece of flounder for lunch today.
- Kohl's after dinner. Tommy got a new suit.
- And he said I can borrow the tie.

DAB – AUGUST 25, 2016

- The nurse at the eye Dr. put drops in Tom's eyes and told him to dab. So he did...

She laughed and said "Second kid to do that today."

GREAT THINGS HAPPEN EVERY DAY

HUMOR HELPS YOU SLEEP – SEPTEMBER 18, 2017

- Tom passed his OA Brotherhood test.
- Got home from camp ahead of schedule.
- Family reunion at Beth's parents.
- Great food.
- Great wine.
- Lots of laughs.
- Finished up the day by watching some Big Bang Theory.

    I read recently that ending the day with a good laugh helps get better sleep, which in turn makes you healthier. I haven't tested it to see, but I know that we finish most nights by watching a sitcom (usually a rerun of "Big Bang Theory", although sometimes it's "Seinfeld" or "Everybody Loves Raymond"). And most nights I sleep really well.

    Of course I also sleep well on nights we watch something on the History Channel or TLC – neither of which are noted for humor. That said, sometimes I laugh at "Ancient Aliens" and "Expedition Unknown". The latter features Josh Gates, who is intentionally funny. The former features Giorgio – who has really funny hair.

FINGER CIRCLE – SEPTEMBER 24, 2018

- I played Daniel Kain at the Harmony Hill historical cemetery tour.
- I only (momentarily) forgot two lines - which I blamed on being dead for over 150 years.
- Got a cool weather run in.
- Paige Craig made us lasagna for dinner.

    I volunteered to get dressed up in costume and play one of the early citizens of our town for a historical society tour. I even posed for a picture.

E-mail me if you looked... phil@philbarthspeaks.com

HUMOROUS COUPONS – SEPTEMBER 26, 2017

- Grilled chicken, veggies and fruit salad for dinner.
- Beth made some chocolate muffin bread - it gets its own spot on the list.
- Frozen yogurt for a bedtime snack.
- Lunch with my friend Marcie - great to catch up.
- Egg white omelet for lunch at First Watch.
- Worked on my upcoming EMUG presentation.

So Wednesday is my colonoscopy. Some may consider this TMI - but it's also something I recommend for everyone over 50. The real question is: What's so funny about that?

Well... For one thing, yesterday we bought the prep products at Meijer. As usual, at checkout we got coupons for related products. In this case - we got a coupon for Glade.

COLONOSCOPY – SEPTEMBER 28, 2017

- Got up at 3:15 to finish my scope prep. Okay, that wasn't a great thing, but I was able to get right back to sleep after.
- The scope itself came back fine.
- Got a good nap during (and for probably a half hour after) the procedure.
- Beth made chicken salad for lunch when we got home.
- Then I got another 1 1/2 hour nap after lunch.
- Made a few calls and got some work stuff done after the nap.
- Taco night for dinner! - Post dinner nap (maybe 10 minutes).
- I wrote a quick blog post about the scope procedure. Just to make sure everyone knows what one is... and yeah there might be a joke or two related to the procedure (you've been warned).

If you just want more information about the procedure, stop after the ALL CAPS line. If, on the other hand, you grew up with me and/or have a similar sense of humor as me, go for the second half of the story.

http://www.philbarthspeaks.com/2016/09/the-scope.html

Bottom line (pun intended) on colonoscopies: The prep is awful. But if I hadn't done my first one 11 years ago I wouldn't be here now.

SIRI ISSUES – OCTOBER 5, 2016

- Chopped tuna salad for dinner.
- Quick but good workout in the fitness center.
- Read more of the Levitt / Dubner book "When to Rob a Bank" (They're the Freakanomics guys - always interesting).
- More progress on my Seattle keynote.
- Found out that iOS 10 has a Siri voice with an Irish accent
- I've been waiting for this!

This is what happens when you don't pay close enough attention to your iPhone settings. I set the Siri voice to Irish, and was then disappointed for two reasons: It didn't sound any different to me than English, and Siri's performance wasn't as good.

I attributed the latter to the iOS upgrade. In reality both were attributable to the fact that I changed the input language for Siri to Irish, so she was expecting ME to speak with an Irish accent.

Everyone was disappointed.

THE NEW VEGETABLE BRUSH – NOVEMBER 7, 2016

- Watched "Mysteries of the Museum" - fun history stories.
- As I left for home I got a message from Beth "I'm feeling better and working on the sweet potatoes. Do you know where my vegetable brush is?"
- A few minutes later I was at Meijer buying a new vegetable brush.
- An OXO one at that.

Beth loves OXO good grips kitchen items. But that wasn't why I bought her a vegetable brush. The truth was this: After she asked I sent her back a message asking what her vegetable brush looked like.

Answer: It's round with a white handle.

I quickly flashed back to a few days earlier when Beth was laid up from surgery and I was "running" the house. In between taking loads of laundry to the washer and dryer I heard the cat throwing up. I grabbed a carpet cleaning brush and some chemicals, scrubbed up the hairball and move on.

Only it wasn't a carpet cleaning brush.

It was a round brush with a white handle.

The great thing: Meijer carries OXO vegetable brushes.

TOM MEETS ICKEY WOODS – DECEMBER 15, 2017

- The moon was almost full on the drive in.
- Ran four miles on the treadmill.
- My friend Andrew showed me how to add things like confetti and fireworks to iMessages.
- Tom got to meet Ickey Woods at the mall.
- Tom asked Ickey "Did you get the cold cuts?"

The next summer we were at the Ohio State Fair, and Tom saw Ickey. He immediately showed him the home screen on his phone, which happened to be the picture above.

THE 100 YEARS NERF DART WAR - DECEMBER 18, 2016

- Nerf war with Joe and Tommy. This is like the 100 years war, only way more fun.
- I found a good joke for announcements at church. It played well.
- Walked at the YMCA for 30 minutes.
- Listened to my book "The Art of the Startup 2.0" by Guy Kawasaki

I couldn't say with any authority that our Nerf dart war was more fun that the 100 years war. I just assumed that to be the case. For all I knew that war made the years 1337 to 1453 a rollicking good time. (And yes, the 100 years war lasted 116 years).

So I watched a YouTube video that billed itself as "A 3-minute summary of the 100 years war". The video actually ran 4:47, but the war ran over too.

Bottom line: England and France fought. A lot of kings died, more kings fought to secede the dead kings. Some kings were infants, some were crazy.

The war was interrupted by the Black Death. When halftime is a rat plague - that's not a lot of fun. Joan of Arc helped the French come back from a near loss. She got burned at the stake. They had no wifi.

Now I can say it with more authority: nerf wars are way more fun. Maybe they would have had more fun in the 100 years war if they had nerf darts.

CHRISTMAS COOKIES - DECEMBER 22, 2016

- After breakfast I went to the Y and got a good run in. This helped offset some of the rest of the day.
- Had turkey soup for lunch at my in laws.
- Then we did the annual traditional cookie decorating, which included my wonderful Cleveland Browns cookie (photo below).
- Then we went to the Old Firehouse Brewery for flights of beer or orange soda. And indoor cornhole.
- My father in law and I won. Decisively.

GREAT THINGS HAPPEN EVERY DAY

Two notes: As I write this book the Browns are no longer (far and away) the worst team in football. This means I have one less source of humor. I'm fine with that.

Also, my father in law and I are not normally great corn hole players. In fact, we fell behind 7-0. But we suddenly got hot, and wound up winning 21-7.

HUMOR

12 | DAD JOKES

I have been a fan of puns for as long as I can remember. In High School our Spanish teacher Mr. Bird was a pun master. I remember at least one Spanish pun (this is dated, but here it goes).

A lady is at the funeral of her husband and she is standing at the casket crying "Por que? Por que?" All of the sudden the casket opens up and says "Butter".

Explanation (if needed) is available at https://www.youtube.com/watch?v=IVWQYeiB6JI

And now one from Mr. Bird that is less dated:

"My handyman finished my boat this week. I told him 'You did a great job. Take a bow'. So he did. But I couldn't be stern with him. So I put the other half up for sale."

In college my roommate Brad and I were pun masters. I don't remember many of them (for a variety of reasons), but I do remember we were frequently lonely.

Eventually we both became fathers. Once you become a dad puns are expected. In fact, they are a badge of honor.

They even have a special title: Dad jokes.

So when I told Joe that Kenny took the bus up from Northern Kentucky and Joe asked "How does he get down?" I was NOT about to tell him the mode of transportation.

The dad requirement was to answer "K.C. and The Sunshine Band".

I still share "Dad jokes" with Mr. Bird on Facebook, and Brad on Twitter.

Somehow that seems backwards. I would expect the tweets to come from Mr. Bird.

A DAD JOKE AT KOHL'S - JANUARY 26, 2018

Tom got in the elevator at Kohl's and said "I think I'm coming down with something." I said "Me too (pause). This elevator!"

TRUNK OR TREAT - OCTOBER 31, 2016

- Spinach salad with goat cheese for lunch.
- Listened to an episode of the Freakanomics podcast - I always recommend that.
- Gave away about 600 pieces of candy at Trunk or Treat.

Each year our church hosts Trunk or Treat. If the weather is good we actually open the trunks (or in the case of SUVs the backs) of our vehicles and kids come through and get candy from each trunk. Plus we generally have a bouncy house and hot dogs on the grill.

If the weather is not nice, we move things indoors. Except for the bouncy house. That wouldn't work.

I like Trunk or Treat because it's fun for the kids, and because I get to dress up in costumes, like this one.

Chicken... cord... on blue.

AS WE LEFT CHURCH TODAY I SAW A LOAF OF BREAD SWADDLED IN A MANGER. I SAID "WHY IS THAT THERE?" TOM SAID "THAT'S THE YEAST OF MY CONCERNS!"

COWS IN THE YARD LEAD TO PUNS – NOVEMBER 9, 2017

- Tommy got a cool new button from Andy Creighton.
- The button gave me an idea for a new vlog episode.
- Beth is down to one crutch around the house.
- Finished reading the book "The Anatomy of Peace".

- Got to see a cow walking through our back yard. Right next to the deck. Soooo close to the grill...
- Made a pun about it, because that's what I do:

A COW JUST WALKED THROUGH OUR YARD. THIS IS THE SECOND TIME IT'S HAPPENED IN THE PAST FIVE YEARS. AT FIRST I THOUGHT IT WAS A RARE OCCURRENCE, BUT NOW I'D SAY IT'S MEDIUM-RARE.

WE USED OUR EXTRA 15% OFF OLLIE'S COUPON. I BOUGHT 100 CALORIE SNACK PACKS. SO NOW THEY ONLY HAVE 85 CALORIES.

GREAT JOKES FROM JOE – OCTOBER 2, 2017

- Helped clean up the community as part of Serve the Burg.
- Grilled burgers for dinner. Tom did the cooking. We also made sautéed mushrooms and turkey bacon for the burgers.
- Joe shared a bunch of silly jokes with us, including my favorite
- Did you hear about the magician in a car who turned in to a driveway?

Another great joke from Joe: A mite is sitting on a fly's back. The fly says "Are you a mite?" The mite says "I might be." The fly says "That's a terrible pun". The mite says "What do you expect? I made it up on the fly!"

HOMEWORK HELP - DECEMBER 17, 2018

- I'm helping Tom study for chemistry. Helping defined as pointing out things like:
- Polar bonds hold together large white arctic bears, and
- You don't want to drink Iodine+Carbon+Uranium, because you could wind up in the ICU.

MORE COW PUNS - SEPTEMBER 19, 2018

- Finished writing my speech "What's on TV?". It will be delivered at the BTC club tomorrow.
- That makes seven speeches written since Chicago.
- Came up with a story idea for speech #8, but I'm not sure what the point is, so it might just sit in my story file for a while.
- Posted about cows, which led to pundemonium.

Not a fan of puns? Just mooove on to the next page.

The post: I wrote a speech about cows. Hopefully it will moooove my audience.

The best of the replies:
It will if you milk it.
You've reached the tipping point.
Sounds like a lot of bull...
You better, or they'll hoof it out of there.
You cud do worse.
I herd your speech was awesome.
You should do comedy – you would be out standing in your field. (My reply: Hay! Great idea).
Do whatever you want. I don't have a steak in the outcome.

(AT RED LOBSTER) WHEN YOU ASK ME WHERE ROCK LOBSTERS COME FROM THERE IS A 100% CHANCE I WILL SAY "THE B-52S".

AIRPORT HUMOR - AUGUST 10, 2018

- Announcement at the airport: "our lounge is a comfortable place to rest and spend time with family before departing." I thought that was a hospice.
- Response from Mr. Bird: I walked by and heard someone coffin.

13 | PETS

We have three family pets. An eleven year old cat (Samantha), a seven year old chocolate lab girl (Bailey), a two year old black (or maybe meth) lab boy (Jesse).

We got Jesse after I had started writing Great Things. A lot of the entries here are around him. It's not that I like him better than the cat, it's just that you can only say "Cat slept on our bed" so many times.

THE NEW PUPPY – JANUARY 7, 2017

- Earlier this week, our deal to get a black lab puppy fell through. The litter was smaller than expected.
- Beth looked around for another breeder, but we kept striking out.
- Yesterday my father in law delivered firewood for our uncle John.
- Since he finished early, he decided to go to the Bethel feed mill (to get cow food).
- When he walked in to the feed mill, a lady was walking out with a black lab puppy.
- He asked her where she got it, and she told him she was a breeder, and had a litter of black lab puppies for sale.
- He got the number, Beth called, we went to see the puppies, and we will have one next week!

THE NEW PUPPY COMES HOME – JANUARY 15, 2017

- We picked up our new doggie!
- Then we spent the rest of the day playing with him.
- And he did some Facebook Live.
- 30 minutes on the stationary bike.
- One hour nap.

PUPPY POO – JANUARY 26, 2017

(If you aren't a fan of puppy poo you might want to move on).

- Jesse and Bailey worked together and removed a plastic ring from the bottom of her bowl.
- When we found the ring there was a 1-inch piece missing.
- 10:30pm last night: Plastic-less puppy poo.
- 2:30am: More plastic-less puppy poo. And now one more great thing:
- At 8:58 this morning I got a call from Beth. Puppy poo with plastic!

    I love dogs. But wow are they gross.

EVERYONE LOVES A NEW PUPPY... WELL ALMOST EVERYONE – JANUARY 29, 2017

- Dinner at Beth's sister Paige's house. Spaghetti and meatballs and homemade bread!
- 30 minutes on the stationary bike.
- I took a nap.
- While the puppy took a nap on me.

Is the puppy gone yet?

MORE PUPPY PICS - JANUARY 30, 2017

- My designer sent me the proof for my book cover. It looks fantastic!
- Four mile run (well walk / run) on the treadmill.
- Waffles for dinner. I made a waffle turkey sandwich, a waffle soy butter and jelly sandwich, and, just to be different, had a waffle with syrup.
- Puppy slept till 5:15.

- Then he got up, went outside and did a quick bio break, and went back to sleep.

Cute now... but not really cute at 5:15.

PUPPY CHECK UP – FEBRUARY 4, 2017

- Kenny, Tommy Beth and I had Chipotle for dinner.
- Beth took the puppy to the vet for booster shots.
- He is gaining 2 lb per week.
- (The puppy, not the vet.)
- But he still fits on my lap in the morning.
- (Also the puppy, not the vet.)

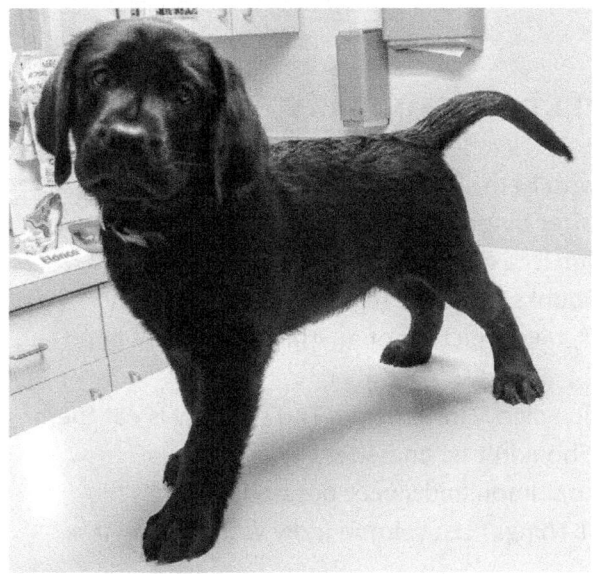

MORE GROSS DOG TALES – FEBRUARY 8, 2017

- Beth made Jesse a chew toy out of an old bandana.
- Bailey ate the bandana.
- Bailey threw up the bandana.
- Jesse needs a new chew toy.

   I love dogs, but once again: They are gross.

THE JOY OF HAVING A PUPPY – MARCH 4, 2017

- Jesse (the puppy) barks around 5am to get up and go outside.
- I take him outside and he quickly does his business.
- We go back inside, and he sits down on the floor.
- I sit down next to him, and he crawls up on my lap.
- I pet him for five minutes while he yawns.
- Then I put him back to bed, and we both get to sleep one more hour.

SALMON AND SWEET POTATO JERKY – MARCH 5, 2018

- Dinner at O'Charley's with Beth, Tommy and Joe. I had salmon.
- Joe went to a concert after dinner. Beth, Tommy and I went to Ollie's and made good use of our 15% off everything coupon.
- I got some grilling cookbooks for $2.99 (less 15%). The strategy is - read through the recipes, take a picture of anything that looks good, then donate the books.
- I also got some Pumpkin Spice Mini Wheats. The strategy is eat them before June (exp date). Shouldn't be an issue.
- And I got the dogs some salmon and sweet potato jerky.
- And if they did a "Great Things" List salmon jerky would be on it.

Ollie's Outlet ("Good Stuff Cheap") is perhaps the only place I can find salmon and sweet potato jerky dog treats. When Beth first saw it she thought it was for me. To be fair, the bag didn't make it clear that it was for dogs. In fact, when I first saw it I thought "Hey, sounds good!" But when I realized it was for dogs, I got them a bag.

It was a huge hit. With the dogs. To be clear, once I realized it was for dogs, I never considered tasting it.

Not because I'm a snob, but because I've been burned on that sort of thing before. Kenny and I tried chicken flavored dog treats once, just to see what they tasted like. (Kenny had previously tried beef flavored dog treats and found them quite tasty).

It was one of those "I will if you will" type dares. We split one in half, took a bite and spit it out. The dogs got the rest of those treats.

DOGS AND CACTI – MARCH 31, 2017

- Watched some TED talks on memory. I forget the titles.
- OK, seriously - the one was a guy who solved a Rubik's cube blindfolded.
- Had a quick conversation with the vet's assistant. The quick conversation with the vet's assistant:

PHIL: IS CACTUS TOXIC TO DOGS? THE INTERNET SAID NO.
ASSISTANT: I DON'T THINK SO, BUT KEEP AN EYE ON HIM.
PHIL: IF I WAS GOOD AT KEEPING AN EYE ON HIM THE CACTUS WOULD STILL BE ALIVE...

NEW RUG / DOG BED – MARCH 29, 2016

- Joe's successful wisdom teeth removal
- Joe on pain meds = quotable quotes.

JOE (GIVING RILEY A CHEESE IT): HEY RILEY – WHO'S MORE BAKED RIGHT NOW, THIS CHEESE CRACKER OR ME?

- 30 minutes on the stationary bike tonight.
- The fact that I was able to catch my mistake on the prior item and not have people thinking I was riding a bike made out of fancy paper.
- Cold grilled chicken for a snack. I like all kinds of leftovers cold - but chicken might be my favorite.
- Getting a new hearth rug with our Kohl's cash. Or Bailey's new bed depending on your point of view...

GREAT THINGS HAPPEN EVERY DAY

14 | GREAT MOMENTS, GREAT PEOPLE

Throughout my life I've met a lot of fun people, and had a lot of enjoyable experiences. Until I started writing "Great Things" I never realized how many great people I was meeting, and how many cool things I was getting to do. Here are some of them:

CALLING IN TO THE RADIO – JANUARY 2, 2017

- Finished the Kindle version of my Cleveland sports book and submitted it to Amazon. It should be up for pre-order in a couple of days.
- Got all the Christmas stuff put away.
- Organized my steins, the tree and lights before I put them away.
- Left bread crumbs so I know how to put things back together next year.
- Talked with Michael Davis.
- Called in to a radio show hosted by Michael's son Brendan and talked about New Year's Resolutions.

Michael Davis (www.speakingcpr.com) is my public speaking coach. And he's a great one. He's also a great friend. We talk sports frequently. He's a Cincinnati fan. I'm from Cleveland so he verbally abuses me during football season. I return the favor during baseball season.

Michael's son needed people to call in to the station and discuss resolutions. I was glad to help. We set it up ahead of time. The best resolution was to get tickets to a monster truck show.

When I called I said "I gave up going to large events like monster truck shows." I then talked about an accidental New Year's resolution I made one year after celebrating (way) too much on New Year's Eve.

OUR ROCK AND ROLL OPTICIAN – JANUARY 8, 2017

- Beth and I got our new glasses.
- The optician that took care of us told us about his hobby - he gets pictures of himself with rock stars: He had pictures with Ringo Starr, Keith Richards and a bunch of others.
- We both made it to 10,000 steps. I had to walk around the house for 5 minutes before bed, but I made it!
- Beth made banana bread.
- It was awesome.

I don't even know how we got on the subject, but the optician showed us pictures of him and Ringo Starr, Keith Richards, and one that was probably the Holy Grail of all rock stars: Bob Dylan. He told us stories of who was friendly, and who was not. Even more fun, he told us how he managed to talk some rock stars in to getting a photo with him.

All in all, it made buying glasses a fun experience. Since that time we've been back for glasses on multiple occasions. And we always check in with the same optician. At one point he said "I need to write a book". I said "You should! I did. It's easy." Then I told him how to do it on Amazon.

As of yet he hasn't written the book. But he keeps adding photos to his collection. And we keep coming back to see them (and buy glasses).

HQ TRIVIA – JANUARY 21, 2018

- Tommy and I played HQ Trivia - we got the first 10 questions right (out of 12).
- That means we came within one question of splitting the $10,000 (Missed #11, but would have gotten #12 right).
- To be clear: Splitting the $10,000 with all other winners - so it would have been approximately $20.
- But - it was a lot of fun.
- Speaking of messages, I received a FB message from a Cleveland sports fan in Germany who enjoyed my book.
- Which of course means my book is now an international best seller (if we define best seller as "best-selling book written by a Cleveland sports fan living in Afton Ohio... ")

Tom and I started playing HQ in January. After a number of close calls I finally won a game, and then a few more along the way. I don't mean to brag, but as I write this my HQ winnings balance is $22. Or maybe 25 cents per hour.

BOOK RELEASE – FEBRUARY 7, 2017

- This might be a day or so late, but Michael Ireland came up with a brilliant cover for my book.
- I got to spend quality time with Tommy, Kenny and Joe. Some yesterday, and some the day before (while watching "Family Guy". Don't judge me.)
- And I got to spend some quality time with the puppy at 3:30 today.
- And 5:30.
- But I'm over it.
- Besides, this isn't sarcastic great things...
- I got 9200 steps. (But this isn't pretty good things).

- Doesn't matter. The awesome book cover and the laughs with my sons still made it a great day.

Michael Ireland is a fellow long suffering Cleveland fan (is there any other kind?).

We first met in Toastmasters. I gave a speech that recounted the misery of being a Cleveland fan (The book also recounts it).

Michael started his evaluation by saying "Damn you Phil! You opened all of those wounds again!"

Michael is also a fantastic designer (see above). You can find him at http://michaelirelanddesign.com/

THE BIG DREAMER – FEBRUARY 9, 2017

- My friend Greg Walker, aka the Big Dreamer, is neighbors with Jimmy Cleamons, the point guard from the 1976 "Miracle of Richfield" Cavaliers. - So Greg gave Jimmy a copy of Hard to Believeland.
- AND... he got me a voice message from Jimmy!
- The message confirmed what I remembered about the Cavs from that era:

"WE DIDN'T CARE WHO GOT THE GLORY" - JIM CLEAMONS.

- This is why seven guys averaged double figures, all between 10 and 16 points per game.
- And it's why they beat the Bullets in the playoffs, and nearly beat the Celtics.
- And it's why I became a Cavaliers fan.
- Thanks Greg Walker! You rock!

Greg Walker, aka the Big Dreamer is an author and motivational speaker and a good friend of mine. He overcame a terrible beginning and became a big success. He now spends his time helping others. Check out his story at https://www.greginspires.com/

PUPPET SHOWS AND COOL SCIENCE – MARCH 16, 2017

- Cool puppet show at our Pack Meeting. Thanks Krista for making it happen!
- I think the adults liked it as much as the kids.
- That was by design: 70s and 80s music throughout.
- And now I'm looking for Mr. Roboto on my iPad.

- And The Banana Boat song.
- And YMCA.
- At any rate - that will be a hard act to follow.
- Unless of course next month's presenter has access to dry ice, liquid nitrogen and things that blow up.
- Fortunately... He does.

Our company has a program called "Seeds of Knowledge". We go to schools and demonstrate "cool science" as a way to get kids interested in STEM. One of the modules we present is called States of Matter. We use dry ice and liquid nitrogen to change things from solids to liquids to gasses. And we bust up roses after putting them in liquid nitrogen. And we turn apples into hammers and drive nails.

The most fun of all comes at the end. We take a lit match to a balloon filled with carbon dioxide (it gives a slight pop).

Then we take a lit match to a balloon filled with nitrogen (another slight pop).

Then we take a lit match to a balloon filled with hydrogen. And that's where science and history (Hindenberg) come together.

FAMILY REUNIONS AND LOCAL MEXICAN RESTAURANTS – MARCH 11, 2018

- Grether family reunion dinner at Rincon.
- I had tacos Rincon, which were delicious.
- Plus Beth shared some of her chicken burrito.
- Got to laugh and have fun with a bunch of great people.
- Beth's sister Paige put a hurt on the margaritas. Or at least we accused her of that.
- Figured out how to beat Daylight Savings Time by falling asleep on the couch early.

Beth's mom's side of the family gets together twice a year. Once is the family reunion at the end of the summer. This takes place at Beth's parents' house, in the front yard, underneath shade trees. Everyone brings food and drinks to share. More on that later.

In the winter the family gets together and gets a huge table at Rincon Mexicano, Authentic Mexican Restaurant and Cantina. The food is delicious and in the case of tacos Rincon, fairly healthy.

The margaritas are giant. I had none. But there were some in our party that enjoyed one. (Those people who had drivers).

I won't begin to claim that Rincon has the market cornered on giant margaritas. There is another local Mexican restaurant – El Rancho Grande – that also has giant margaritas. And it also has delicious food.

THE ELOPING COUPLE – MARCH 21, 2018

- Beth and I hit Meijer after dinner.
- But the Meijer in Eastgate had no power.
- So we hit the Meijer in Milford.
- It took longer, but we got everything.
- And the couple behind us in the checkout line had all kinds of interesting travel items - dramamine, books, swim goggles, suntan lotion.
- When Beth said "Are you going some place fun?"
- They said "We're eloping!"

Reason #32867 why I love my wife: Sometimes I get caught up in my own little world. But she notices cool things like the couple behind us with all kinds of vacation stuff. So she talks with them. And we get to hear a great story.

THE LEGO STORE – MARCH 25, 2016

- Trip to the Kenwood Towne Center.
- Tommy got a lego set.
- So did I. (A desk calendar)
- We also hit the LL Bean store and found some cool stuff.
- Tom tested one of the Adirondack chairs for napping. It passed.

My lego set:

DAN NAINAN - APRIL 14, 2018

- Exit row with no one next to me, and no row right in front of me either. It happened on both flights
- Breakfast at the Atlanta airport: Salmon and egg sandwich.
- I was able to scrape the avocado off the sandwich before I ate it.
- Two words: Airplane nap.
- Woke up from my nap just in time to get Kenny's biscoff cookies (when I travel I'm Kenny's cookie mule).
- Got one ton of gravel down on the driveway.
- Attended a really good humor webinar that had a guest star - the hilarious Dan Nainan.

- Had a homemade smoothie.
- The greatest thing: being back at home and in my own bed.

Dan Nainan (www.dannainan.com) is a hilarious 100% clean comedian. I was fortunate enough to meet him in Las Vegas when he headlined the Toastmasters convention in 2011. And I have been fortunate enough to trade football jokes with him many times since (when you're a Browns fan you have plenty of material, or at least I did until mid-2018.)

FRIENDS FROM AROUND THE WORLD – MAY 9, 2016

- On the flight to Atlanta I listened to a Ziglar podcast from March - an interview with Kevin Kruse (15 secrets successful people know about time management). I learned a lot.
- Salmon salad at Atlanta for lunch.
- Was on a flight with several Memphis based co-workers to Wilmington - which meant I got an invite to hang out with some really great people at dinner.
- Not only people from Memphis, but also Europe, China, Japan and Brazil.
- More salmon at dinner. Poor fish.. I'm on a mission...
- I sat next to my buddy Andrew at dinner, which meant I got to learn new things, like FOMO, selling Buicks, and a new pulp concept.

One of the great things about working with our global sales force is meeting people from around the world. We get to learn about each other's cultures and customs.

But sometimes it's fun to learn what we have in common. The first time I met our sales manager from Tokyo we talked about baseball. He complained that his favorite team in the Japanese League (Nippon Professional Baseball) hadn't won a championship in about ten years.

Then I told him about the Cleveland Indians (no championship since 1948). And we learned another universal truth – pain is funny.

OUR CHEF MIKE, THE FELLOW CLEVELAND SPORTS FAN – MAY 12, 2017

- Sizzling salad for lunch: Shrimp, veggies, lettuce, garlic, pepper, vinegar and oil.
- Talked with Mike (the chef at our cafeteria and a fellow Cleveland sports fan) while he made the salad.
- Found out that Mike also had a heart attack a few years back. Wait - that's not a great thing - but it was great to see he has fully bounced back.
- Found out that Dan Nainan is doing a guest voice on Family Guy this month. I'm watching.
- Beth made spaghetti for dinner.
- I had seconds.
- 30 minutes on the elliptical.
- Answered two questions for Randy Lampe, which brings my weekly total to... two.

Our chef at work grew up in Cleveland. He had a job as a sous chef in Richfield. He got to meet several of the Cleveland Cavaliers over the years. This was back when they played at the Richfield Colosseum. At any rate, we discussed Cleveland sports on many occasions.

Unfortunately, over half of our campus moved out, and they had to close down the cafeteria. Before we did, I gave him a copy of the "Hard to Believeland" Book. He had no idea I had written it.

(Well, it sold about 200 copies… so I understand how he might have missed it).

CLOCK TOWER – JULY 26, 2017

- Beth and I went to dinner at Camp Friedlander, where I had:
- Pulled pork and a really great salad and strawberry shortcake.
- Picked blackberries with Tom.
- 30 minutes on the elliptical - made my back feel better (the bike ride yesterday hurt it a bit).
- Listened to one of the recording Kenny made. It's called Clock Tower and it's awesome. - I know I'm biased, but it's awesome. (And I can be biased and right).
- Finished day with an after dark "man bath" in the pool.

https://www.youtube.com/watch?v=VULd-0tBOVY

This became the lead in for all of my speaking videos and Tom and my Great Things Vlog videos

WILLIE MAE – NOVEMBER 10, 2016

This is Willie Mae. Of all the happy people working at Embassy Suites in Memphis she is the happiest and nicest. She sings good morning to everyone. She is happy to bus the tables, and she makes customers happy too. Her great attitude is contagious!

A lady at another breakfast table said "Oh. You must be a morning person." Willie Mae smiled and said "I'm an all day person!" I'm grateful for Willie Mae (and not just because her name is easy to remember #sayhey #greatthings)

GREAT THINGS HAPPEN EVERY DAY

15 | MISCELLANEOUS STORIES

When I first started "Great Things" we were on Spring Break. We had something big planned every day. A trip to the zoo, a trip to the museum, picnic in the park. At the time I wondered how long I would be able to keep finding big things to put in the Great Things blog. It turned out we didn't need to do something big or even something new to experience a great thing. Some of the greatest moments are just a quick slice of life. For example:

LITTLE GUY HELPS ME IN THE ELEVATOR – APRIL 13, 2016

- Morning workout at the Hilton Fitness Center.
- Another free breakfast.
- Great tour of the new machine at the mill.
- Got a nice pair of waterproof steel toed work boots at Wal Mart.
- Listened to the Tim Ferriss podcast: "How to avoid the busy trap"
- Found an easier way in and out from the parking lot to my room.
- Scottish salmon for dinner. Not sure what that means exactly, but it was good.
- Walked to and from dinner - wound up with 12,000 steps.
- Got to bed early so I can get up bright and early tomorrow and fly home! Okay I haven't done that one yet, but I will soon

I missed one of the really fun things that happened yesterday on my great things list. I got on the elevator with a family. The young boy said "Dad - can I press 6?" His dad said okay. After he hit 6, I said "Hey buddy - can you press 4 for me?" He looked at his mom and dad and they nodded. "SURE!" A little while later the elevator stopped and he said "Here's 4!"

HIGH TECH MOM – FEBRUARY 10, 2017

- Learned a lesson about when to call a plumber vs. try something myself.
- Fortunately the cut didn't require more than a band aid.
- And the blood came out of my shirt.
- Pain free dentist appointment / checkup.
- Talked with my mom on the phone (not during the dental check up).
- She now has high speed wifi. - And YouTube access! I might get up to 100 hits on my speech yet!

I love that my mom, at age 80, still learns technology. It's a great way to keep young. She has an iPad, high speed wifi, YouTube and Instagram. Not bad! #onedayyounger

CAMPING WITH A CPAP - APRIL 22, 2017

- Made it to General Butler State Park.
- Sat by the fire pit.
- Put up tents with Tom and Joe.
- Watched as Joe made several scouts laugh out loud.
- Put my tent up by the electrical outlet. I won't need the inverter for my CPAP.

Some campouts we have an electrical outlet. In those cases I can plug my CPAP in directly (I run an extension cord from the tent). There are other cases, however, where we don't have an electrical outlet option. In those cases I bring along a Schumacher inverter. I picked it up at Wal Mart before our trip to Sea Base.

I also have a ResMed DC converter (about $82 on Amazon). The price is terrible, but it's a CPAP. Low prices don't happen. When I use the DC converter I can get four to five days of CPAP usage from the inverter.

ATLATL – MAY 21, 2016

- Woke up at our campout with birds singing. Went back to sleep.
- Had Farmer's Breakfast for lunch.
- Over 15,000 steps.
- Learned about the Fort Ancient Indians.
- Spent lots of time with Beth and Tommy.
- Threw the atlatl and showed my troop who the man was!
- Took a nap.
- Evening fire.

An Atlatl is an ancient hunting weapon. It's also known as a spear thrower. The atlatl is basically a wooden extension of the arm. The arm and atlatl work as a giant lever, allowing the hunter (or in my case the scoutmaster) to throw the spear (or in my case a wooden stick) a long distance. And I still don't know how I did it, but we had a garbage can across the field as our target. And I was the first one to hit it. I immediately quit. I decided to let the troop think I was lucky. Had I thrown again they would have known I was lucky.

CAVS WIN IT ALL – JUNE 19, 2016

- Father's Day dinner at my in-law's house.
- Pasta bake from Beth, plus
- Her famous pumpkin pie!
- Lunch with Beth at Panera.
- 30 minutes on the treadmill at the Y.

GREAT THINGS HAPPEN EVERY DAY

- Beth and I dropped Tom off at NYLT - he looked so good - proud of that boy!
- And yeah, I'm watching the finals. It's a great game... But it has the chance to be a REALLY great one...

And so it was. The game featured the #chasedown and #theshot. And it featured the first major league sports championship for Cleveland fans in 52 years.

WAIT! IT WASN'T TRASH! JULY 14, 2016

- Oatmeal for breakfast
- Hilton Wilmington makes great oatmeal.
- Southern food for lunch (Tilapia, cornbread and peach cobbler). The IT manager at our Riegelwood mill gets great catering for lunch.
- Bonefish Grill for dinner - Salmon and veggies.
- Lots of work done today.
- And I did something dumb...

My business trip started with a flight to Charleston, SC. I then drove to Georgetown for meetings at our paper mill. Two days later I drove to Wilmington, NC for meetings at another paper mill. I then flew home from Wilmington.

When I landed in Charleston I had a little time, so I stopped at an antique shop and found a piece of Wedgwood for Beth. I wanted to make sure it got home safely. At one of the mills, I found a box with bubble wrap in it. It was just the right size for the Wedgwood. It was going to be thrown away, so I took it with me. I got back to Wilmington, parked my car and took the box to my room.

(NOTE: Thankfully I had not boxed up the Wedgwood at this point).

When I got to my room I realized I had left my room key back in the car. I didn't feel like taking the box all the way back to the car (My room was a long way from the parking lot). I sat the box down, and walked back to get the key.

Sure enough, by the time I got back to my room, the box had been taken away as trash.

The gift made it home fine. I cleared out space in my briefcase (threw everything in to the checked luggage) and carried it home.

LOVE SURPRISE – JULY 15, 2016

- My love surprise was a homemade peach pie from Beth
- Beth got a piece of Wedgwood from me.
- Kenny got a jumbo Monster energy drink from Joe
- Joe got a 4 pack of Mountain Dew with real sugar from Tommy.
- Tommy got a 12 pack of Mountain Dew from Kenny.
- And tonight the boys and I are going to the Reds game. - We're in the Party Deck!
- (Party on Wayne... Party on Barth... #dadjoke... sorta)

One of our great family traditions is the Love Surprise. Each person secretly gets another family member a surprise gift that says "I love you". (Names are drawn at random).

We draw at the start of the week and give the gifts at the end of the week.

ANOTHER GREAT TRADITION - SPECIAL SCOOP

Beth started this years ago. She bought a scoop at a Flea Market. At dinner she announced that we would take turns having the scoop (one person each day). The person with the scoop says grace for the meal. During the meal, everyone else at the table says something they appreciate about that person. The idea is to make it something recent.

Something like "I appreciate you played Super Smash Brothers with me" or "I appreciate you took me to my guitar lesson".

The tradition has survived for years.

THIS WAS THE DAY YOU ALMOST GOT FREE PIZZA – JULY 28, 2018

- Tom and I went to the International Paper Reds game.
- We had a private suite.
- With beer, pop, and a buffet.
- Tom had a bunch of pot stickers.
- I mean a BUNCH of them.
- The Reds struck out a lot of batters early. In fact they got to 10 in the seventh inning.
- That was important because 11 strikeouts in a game gets everyone a free small LaRosa's pizza.
- We figured with the setup guys and the closer coming in, the pizza was in the bag.
- We learned to not count our strikeouts before they hatch.

As noted before, there was a game when our tickets got us free pizza. This wasn't that game. I'll bet there were five or six times when the opposing hitter had two strikes. And every time that batter took a pitch, the crowd yelled at the umpire to ring him up.

Personally, every time the batter made contact I was hoping for a hit, just to give us another shot at a free pizza.

Potential free pizza makes for a bloodthirsty crowd.

MISCELLANEOUS STORIES

LOGGERHEAD TURTLES - AUGUST 24, 2016

- Got to see baby loggerhead turtles walk from their nest to the ocean.
- There were a lot of other cool things, but it's really tough to beat a turtle migration.

We were at a sales dinner near the beach outside of Wilmington, North Carolina. We had walked past the protected nests earlier, but this time we walked out right after sunset. The people who deal with loggerhead turtles had opened up the nest to allow the hatched turtles to walk down a path to the ocean.

Roughly one out of 1,000 will make the journey all the way from the beach in North Carolina, around Africa and back to the same beach.

The key is to get them to the ocean - after dark (when birds can't pick them off).

That's what the Loggerhead people were doing. They open the nest on three consecutive evenings after sundown. Any turtle that hasn't made it out by the end of evening three is taken out to the reef. That turtle won't do the journey, but it will have a better life than being bird food.

HEATED CAR SEATS – MARCH 7, 2017

- Got a rental car while our CRV is in the body shop.
- And it has heated seats!

The rental GMC SUV was a lot of fun to drive. The fuel economy wasn't exactly what we were used to, but the room was nice. And then there were the heated car seats. Driver and passenger, back and bottom, three levels of heat. It isn't terribly cold in March in southern Ohio.

That said, the heated seats were a game changer. And they will be part of every car I buy from now on.

HEATED STEERING WHEEL – MARCH 20, 2017

- Great speech practice at the ACE Toastmasters. Thanks for the hospitality and feedback!
- Got to hear some great speeches, including my friend Carol telling us about her Mercedes.
- On the way home I discovered that the rental car not only has heated seats, but it also has a heated steering wheel.

The best part of the day was hearing Carol talk about her heated steering wheel, then going to the rental GMC SUV and thinking "I wonder…" and finding a heated steering wheel option.

Because if there's one thing better than having a warm back and warm butt, it's having warm hands and not needing gloves. Not that I would have needed gloves on March 20 anyway, but warm hands are nice.

My next car will also have a heated steering wheel.

MOVIES FOR DADS AND SONS – SEPTEMBER 29, 2016

- Back in the office. Got a lot done.
- Salad for lunch.
- 30-minute run.
- Beth made spaghetti for dinner.
- Tom, Beth and I watched Downton Abbey (we're still catching up).
- Then we watched "Young Frankenstein".
- And last night we watched "Top Secret!"

An incomplete list of movies dads should watch with their sons:

Young Frankenstein
Top Secret!
Airplane!
The Naked Gun – 1, 2 ½ and 33 1/3.
Austin Powers – the entire series.
Monty Python and the Holy Grail
A Few Good Men
Shrek
Anything with Indiana Jones.
Pirates of the Caribbean
The Hobbit trilogy.
Field of Dreams
Dirty Rotten Scoundrels
Any movie where Stan Lee makes a cameo appearance.

Do you have a favorite movie suggestion? Send it to me! phil@philbarthspeaks

MOVIE NIGHT, CONTINUED – OCTOBER 1, 2016

- Tom and I got haircuts.
- I watched the Cross Country race at Williamsburg.
- Dinner at Cracker Barrel. I had trout, Lima beans, and what tasted like 2 desserts: Baked Sweet potato and fried apples.
- Target afterwards
- I got some workout shorts at 75% off, and...
- Some pajamas (which I noticed I needed after I organized the closet) for 50% off.
- Tom found some Pikachu sleep shorts.
- And it was movie night featuring: Dirty Rotten Scoundrels.
- Banana milkshakes (Phil and Beth) or chocolate milkshakes (Kenny and Tom) with the movie.

A word of explanation about the prior movie choices: I purposefully said the list was incomplete.

When I posed this question on Facebook, some people suggested movies that were educational. Others suggested movies that would be more suited for older kids.

This is my take: I want a movie where we can sit and laugh together, and be able to post on Facebook that we watched it without people threatening to call child protective services.

Although most of our movies are humor, sci fi or adventure, there are times when we watch movies with a point.

For example: The other night we watched Remains of the Day with Emma Thompson and Anthony Hopkins.

(Spoiler alert)

Tom said "I hated that movie because they didn't end up together in the end."

My reply: "Well, that's the message of the movie. If you don't take action to get what you really want, it won't happen. And then you get upset, wind up being a mass murderer and cannibal".

This was met with disapproval from Beth.

The look became more disapproving when I called her Clarice.

THE BURPING CONTEST – OCTOBER 3, 2016

- Outdoor run in perfect weather.
- Spinach salad with goat cheese and cranberries (all from Jungle Jim's) for lunch.
- Beth made chili spaghetti for dinner.
- Banana milkshakes for bedtime snack.

- Then a glass of raspberry wine.
- I fell asleep on the couch while watching Star Trek the Next Generation.
- And Tom and I made a vlog.

This one comes with a warning: If burps offend or even annoy you, don't watch. It was four minutes of silliness and (of course) burping. I have done over 100 videos with Tom. And the burping one has the most hits. Go figure. The link may not work on your device (or paper book). Or you may not be interested in a burping contest.

If you are interested, and the link does not work, Look up "Phil Barth burping contest" on YouTube. As of this writing, it's the top one. https://youtu.be/G3Ymt6WIByU

TOM'S FIND AT PETERLOON – OCTOBER 8, 2016

- Peterloon. I was unplugged for Friday night, all day Saturday and Sunday morning. I got to spend time with Tom (okay, I wasn't entirely unplugged, we did record some vlog footage on the iPhone).
- We had all kinds of great food, including the mobile Cone, Waffo and Dutch oven lasagna.
- We had perfect weather, and Tom and his buddies had a great weekend.
- Tom won a stuffed animal.

Tom won a stuffed animal at the Gorman farms game. We got it home, and found out it was a used (and likely donated) stuffed frog. Tom cleaned it up, and found out it was actually a talking bullfrog, so he put batteries in it and started playing with it. Meanwhile, Beth looked it up online. It was the hottest toy in 1998 - it goes for $50. Tom needs to become a picker.

Of course the frog goes for $50 new in box, and Tom got it used. That's okay, because Paige offered him $50 for it and he turned her down.

It is pretty cool. You can hold him upside down, tickle his belly, etc, and he says different things. (The frog, not Tom).

TOM'S EAGLE PROJECT FIRE PIT – OCTOBER 23, 2018

- Salvation Army came and picked up all of the leftovers from our Boy Scout rummage sale.
- And a lot of other things.
- We now have a clean garage.
- Tom and I finished installing the benches for his fire pit. All we have left to do is finish the gravel! - Beth, Tommy, Joe and I played HQ "The Office" trivia.
- Well, mostly Joe... I just clicked on the answers he gave me.
- We came close, but didn't win.
- We watched a couple of episodes after the game to improve our chances for the next game.

MISCELLANEOUS STORIES

WORLD SERIES – OCTOBER 28, 2016

Great things that happened today - non-baseball edition:

- Beth and I went to Joe Barth's checkup. All of his numbers are great.
- And he's still not as tall as me.
- We had a lot of laughs, as we always do when Joe is around.
- Tom and I went to Jungle Jim's.
- He found some lego figures he wanted.
- I got apples for 55 cents a lb.
- And pineapples for 99 cents each.

Baseball edition:

- After the Indians didn't score in the first inning I decided to work on a broken cabinet hinge and listen only to the game while the Cubs were batting.
- The Cubs didn't score.
- I took a break to go back to the game when the Indians hit.
- Then I went back to the cabinet when the Cubs hit, listen only.
- After two innings, I decided to keep it going: Watch the Tribe hit, work and listen only when the Cubs were up...
- I wound up fixing two cabinets, posting a flier on Facebook, and freezing 4 gallons worth of apples.
- Oh yeah, the Indians won.
- Now I have to find some things to do tomorrow when the Cubs bat.

The bad news – I ran out of cabinets to fix... and the Indians ran out of wins.

RE-HASHING THE WORLD SERIES – NOVEMBER 3, 2016

- Beth continues to recover from knee surgery..
- Beth's sister provided dinner.
- Rehashed the World Series with my friend Chris.

- While we didn't get the result we wanted we agreed that it was good to get to rehash a World Series for the first time in 19 years.

Looking back on this all I can say is "Yeah right".

The end of the World Series was anything BUT a great thing for Chris and I.

There is much more on this in my book "Hard to Believeland". Fair warning – my summary of the series wasn't pretty.

\

ENTIRE FAMILY FOR DINNER – MAY 6, 2016

- Got an outdoor run in.
- Listened to Zig Ziglar on my run.
- Found some great stuff on sale at Kohl's.
- Beth, Joe and Kenny got a load of mulch down - it looks fantastic!
- Had a grape / strawberry / spinach / blueberry smoothie.
- Nearly finished the book "Killing Reagan".
- Grilled burgers for dinner.
- Had the entire family at the table for dinner.

When the kids were young we were around the table for dinner almost every night. Now Kenny has moved out and Joe has college classes or work many evenings. When we are able to get together as a family it makes it even more special and even more of a great thing.

A GREAT MOMENT FROZEN IN TIME - JULY 7, 2017

- I'm sitting in my recliner, eating a half of a (relatively) low fat and low sodium Old #9 meat stick.
- While I'm sipping on an IPA from the Old Firehouse Brewery.
- My incredible wife Beth is sitting next to me.
- Our cat is sleeping on the chair next to us.
- Our dogs are sleeping on the floor.
- Tommy and I just got back from a swim.
- Before that I picked about a half-gallon of blackberries.
- Before that we had a scout fund raiser at the garden club.

Sometimes it's nice to freeze a moment in time and consider all the great things that are happening around you. That was the case for this particular great things moment.

THE GREATEST OF GREAT THINGS – JULY 6, 2016

- "8 track flashback" when I listened to Boston while riding the stationary bike.
- All five of us went out for dinner.

But the greatest thing that happened today was Kenny, Tom, Phil and grandpa Kenny and I had a "man bath" (another name for late night swimming).

Technically only Tom got in the pool. The rest of us took care of the growler from Kenny's birthday. Joe joined us later.

We told jokes, laughed, and made memories.

And that was the greatest thing that happened today.

A GREAT MOMENT - JANUARY 13, 2019

- I'm sitting across the kitchen table from Beth.
- She is working on Harmony Hill finances.
- I am working on my book.
- Kenny, Joe and their band are practicing downstairs.
- Kenny's girlfriend Vanna and Jesse are asleep on the couch.
- Beth is baking a cake.

16 | CONCLUSION

"Keep your face to the sunshine and you cannot see a shadow" - Helen Keller

I'm not sure I buy the "cannot see a shadow" part of the above quote, at least not 100% of the time. But there are a few things I've learned in four years of looking for the great things in life:

Great things are not the same as great big things. Some of the happiest and greatest moments were very small things. Sitting at a dinner with our entire family. Enjoying a glass of my in-laws homemade wine. Or taking an after dinner walk with Beth. Little things make a difference.

When you look for great things, you will find them. Even better: The more you look for them the more you will find, and the easier it will be to find them. When you train your reticular activating system to find the great things - they will show up all the time.

Corollary: If you're busy looking for great things, it will be more difficult to find bad things. Mind you it's not impossible to find bad things. People will still cut you off in traffic. The wifi will go out when you need it. LeBron James will leave your favorite basketball team again.

When you look for great things, you will find great things in others. When I started looking for great things I found them in people who were different from me. People with different backgrounds. People with different beliefs. People from around the world.

Finding great things in others who are different from you is the first step in finding great things in yourself.

Most importantly: **When you start looking for great things the odds will work in your favor.** (Just like Hunger Games...)

This is thanks to the miracle I like to call "Great Things Math". Here's how it works:

There are a certain number of days in a year that will not be great days, no matter how great your attitude is, no matter how many great things you try to find.

There are also a certain number of days in a year that will be great days, no matter what. (This is not a challenge. I'm certain there are people out there who could win a million dollars and complain that it was given to them in 50s instead of 100s. But those people aren't reading this book.).

Then there are days that could go either way.

If you look for the great things those days will be great ones.

For example:

FLIGHT DELAYS - OCTOBER 26-27 2016

- An hour delay at Memphis, which was a great thing because in that time I...
- Read some more of my book.
- Had dinner at a sit down airport restaurant with (friend and co-worker) Randy. It took a while, but we had time, and the food was great.
- Sat next to a guy on the plane who reminded me why I bring noise canceling headphones on flights.

CONCLUSION

(We now step out for the story):

The guy started talking about how he hadn't had a delay in forever going through Atlanta. (Neither had I - at the time).

Then he proceeded to whine and complain about the fact that we were running an hour behind, and how many times he had experienced such a terrible delay in Memphis (I think the number was three, but I really started paying attention to my book at this point).

THEN... when we exited the plane he made sure to yell at the flight attendant about it because I guess flight attendants control the weather in Cincinnati and/or plane maintenance.

(Back to great things).

- Had a really nice flight crew and a really nice lady at Memphis (who got me upgraded).

Given who I wound up next to on the plane I'm not sure the upgrade was a great thing on this flight. But she updated my profile as well, and the upgrades flowed freely for the remainder of the year.

FLIGHT DELAYS - OCTOBER 26-27 2017

- I got home at from Memphis at 2am.
- The delay wasn't great, but jamming to Little Feat on open roads on the way home from the airport was.
- Dinner at Chili's With Beth, Tommy, and Joe.
- The food was delicious and the service was fantastic.
- We had a bunch of gift cards (or as our waitress said "You're Chili's rich.")
- Trip to Ollie's Outlet and Hallmark.

Two years in row I had meetings in Memphis.
Two years in a row I flew home the day before our wedding anniversary.
Two years in a row we had delays.

(Two years in a row I was flying with my friend and co-worker Randy – he might be a jinx…)

This is the perfect example of a day that could go either way. The guy sitting next to me on October 26, 2016 let it go to the bad side of the ledger. I can't blame him. Before I started looking for great things, I would have done the same thing.

When I started looking for great things, even flight delay days wound up being great days.

I can't promise that every day will be a great day. It didn't work that way for me. But I can promise you this:

The more you look for great things, the more you swing those days to the positive side of the ledger.

If one day per month is bad no matter what and one day per month is good no matter what, you have 29 days up for grabs. Look for great things and make those days great.

Let me conclude by saying what I said at the start of the book

I want to start a movement where we focus on what's great in life. I want to start a lower stress movement. I want to keep one person out of the cardiac wing. I want that person to be you.

I hope you start a list as well. You don't have to put the list on Social Media. You don't even need to write it down. Just think about the great things that happened each day.

As I said before: I'd love to hear from you. If you have a great family tradition, great recipe or any other great moment that makes life more enjoyable - send them to me on Twitter (@philbarthspeaks), or shoot me an e-mail – phil@philbarthspeaks.com. I will in turn share the greatest things on my website (www.philbarth.com)

Together we can do it!

ABOUT THE AUTHOR

Phil Barth has looked at the #greatthings in life for over three years now. He has recorded them on Facebook almost every day, and his blog (www.philbarth.com) when he remembers to do so. His life is dramatically better as a result of this three year quest.

This is Phil's second book, the first being the international seller (no, I didn't accidentally leave out the word "best"… but it did sell a copy in Canada and one in Germany) Hard to Believeland, the story of what it's like to grow up a fan of Cleveland based professional sports. (Spoiler alert, that book is a little different from this one).

Phil, his wife and sons reside in the greater Cincinnati area.

Phil is writing this section, and doesn't like to talk about himself in the third person.

I'd love to hear from you:
Twitter: @philbarthspeaks
Facebook: Phil Barth
www.philbarth.com
phil@philbarthspeaks.com

Made in the USA
Monee, IL
19 November 2021